SKI VERMONT!

SKI VERMONT!

A Complete Guide to the Best Vermont Skiing

A VERMONT LIFE BOOK
By Jules Older

Vermont Life Magazine
Montpelier, Vermont

Chelsea Green Publishing Company
Post Mills, Vermont

Printed in the United States of America. First Edition.

1 2 3 4 5 6 7 8 9 10

Book design by Jan Lowry Hubbard.
Maps copyright © by Walter Vose Jeffries

Library of Congress Cataloging-in-Publication Data
Older, Jules.
   Ski Vermont! / by Jules Older.
     p.   cm.
   Includes bibliographical references.
   ISBN 0-930031-44-X : $14.95
   1. Skis and skiing—Vermont—Guide-books. 2. Ski resorts-
-Vermont—Guide-books. 3. Vermont—Description and travel—1981-
-Guide-books. I. Title.
GV854.5.V5043   1991
796.93'09743—dc20   91-16650

Contents

Preface

Writing a guide to Vermont's ski areas probably sounds like a lot of fun. It is.

From October (Killington opens early) to May (Killington closes late), from the Canadian border (Jay Peak is within hailing distance of Canada) to the Massachusetts line (Haystack is just over the border from the Bay State), from the dawn's early light (because the dawn's early light is the best light for ski photography) to the last rays of dusk (when I'd ride with the groomers in their big Pisten Bullies), I lived Vermont skiing. Together with my photographer-wife, Effin, I covered every major mountain in the state.

I rode the single chair at Mad River Glen, the double at Mount Snow, the triple at Magic, the fast quad at Pico and the even faster gondola at Stratton. I grabbed rides on a Poma lift at Sugarbush, a T-bar at Haystack, a gondola at Stowe and Vermont's only tram at Jay Peak. I took lessons everywhere. I *gave* lessons for a couple of weeks.

In the process of evaluating Vermont skiing I sampled restaurants, pubs, hotel rooms, swimming pools, saunas, health clubs, chairlifts and, of course, ski trails. It was hard — oh, it was hard — but research is demanding work.

Covering the territory between Jay Peak and Haystack I put 4,350 miles on my car without ever leaving the state. I tried to calculate how many miles I'd skied, then how many vertical feet, then how many trails. In the end the numbers overwhelmed me, and when asked about it I'd shrug and mumble, "I — uh — skied a whole lot."

The amount of pleasure I got from skiing Vermont's beautiful mountains would be even harder to calculate. The fact is, I received a whole lot.

As you read this book, I hope you will, too. If you take it along on a Vermont ski trip, I know you will. Because the principle underlying *Ski Vermont!* is the idea that Vermont's many ski areas all have differences — in character and in types of trails — and that when you know those differences you'll be able to select which areas suit you best, and to get more out of skiing those areas. I know that the Green Mountain State will exceed your expectations, as it did mine.

A FEW WORDS OF THANKS

In researching and writing this book, I've been greatly aided by the ski areas of Vermont and by the Vermont Ski Areas Association. They have corrected my mistakes, brought my facts up to date, indicated their pleasure ("The book should be a great success!") and their displeasure ("How can you say that?") with my words. I am grateful for their input, their frankness and their acceptance that the perceptions that ultimately appear in the book are my own.

And that is one of the greatest values of this book: that it gives an inside look at Vermont ski areas beyond the information already available in promotional brochures.

Working with the staff of *Vermont Life* Magazine has been a real bonus in what was already a dream assignment. I thank the staff and particularly editor Tom Slayton for wise counsel, clear guidelines and consistent helpfulness. The book and I owe him a great debt.

I'd also like to acknowledge the debt American skiers owe to those who founded skiing in this country. Some were native-born athletes and entrepreneurs. Many others were foreigners, especially Austrians and Norwegians, who came (and are still coming) to this brash, young country, and who helped lead us up and down the snow-covered mountains. Skiing wouldn't be the same without them.

Finally, my wife, Effin, has accompanied me on every mile of this exciting journey through Vermont and has critically edited every word in this book. My thanks and my love.

Jules Older
May, 1991

SKI VERMONT!

Alpine Ski Areas in Vermont

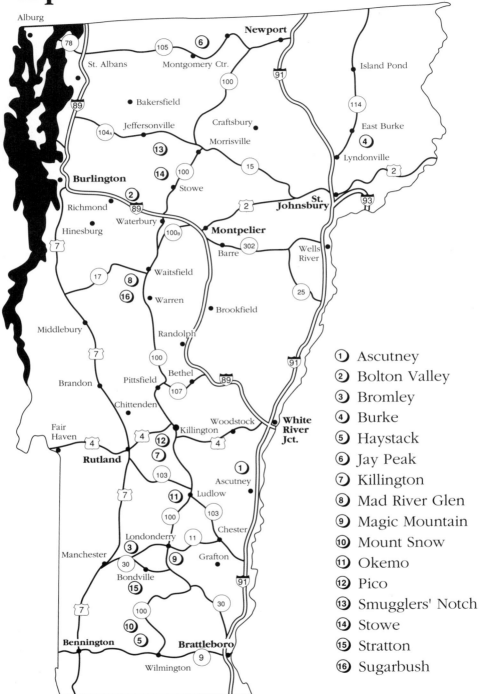

1. Ascutney
2. Bolton Valley
3. Bromley
4. Burke
5. Haystack
6. Jay Peak
7. Killington
8. Mad River Glen
9. Magic Mountain
10. Mount Snow
11. Okemo
12. Pico
13. Smugglers' Notch
14. Stowe
15. Stratton
16. Sugarbush

Introduction

How to Choose the Best Ski Area for You

Because I'm a ski writer, people are always asking me, "What's the best ski area in Vermont?" Sometimes the questioner adopts the conspiratorial tone of one looking for inside information: "C'mon, you can tell me. What's *really* the best ski area in Vermont?"

My answer is always the same: It depends on what you're looking for.

Some folks don't believe me. They think I'm hiding a secret reserved for ski writers. But it's true — the best depends on what kind of best you want.

Here are some of my personal bests.

If you're looking for an old-fashioned area — a bit funky, rugged, narrow-trailed, uncrowded and personal — Burke Mountain, Magic Mountain and Mad River Glen are the best.

For the ego boost that comes from cruising wide trails through intermediate terrain, Ascutney, Bolton Valley, Bromley, Haystack, Okemo and Pico are right up at the top.

If you're looking for hard stuff — challenging trails, moguls, scary pitches — Jay Peak, Mad River, Magic Mountain, Killington, Smugglers' Notch and Stowe will give you your money's worth and then some.

Want instruction? As long as you avoid the busiest weeks of the year (particularly Christmas and Presidents' Day), you'll do fine at any Vermont ski resort. My favorite is Smugglers' Notch, but I may be prejudiced — I occasionally teach there.

Bringing a young family? Again, it's hard to go wrong, since virtually every area offers child care. Near Burlington, Bolton Valley and Smugglers' Notch both have the atmosphere of carless villages. Near Rutland, Pico Peak is a family tradition. Further south, Bromley and Okemo have excellent child care facilities. In the far north, Jay Peak offers great bargains for families.

Got the teenagers with you? Smugglers' and Killington are awesome.

Want something upmarket? It's hard to beat Stratton, Stowe and Sugarbush. Ascutney and Okemo are newer contenders.

Life in the fast lane? K-I-L-L-I-N-G-T-O-N. Vying for second place, Mt. Snow and Stowe.

In the slow lane? Burke Mountain up north and tiny Maple Valley down south.

College atmosphere? Middlebury Snow Bowl all the time and Smugglers' Notch during winter vacations.

Great snow grooming? Okemo, Mt. Snow, Magic Mountain, Stowe — every year more Vermont areas reach excellence in caring for snow.

Exotic, foreign atmosphere? Jay Peak and Mt. Snow. (Both the province of Quebec and New York City are neighbors of the U.S. yet somehow excitingly different.)

The list goes on. In truth, these days it's hard to have a bad time at a Vermont ski area. The lifeblood of skiing is repeat business, and every resort is determined that you have such a good time that you'll want to come back tomorrow.

How do you choose a ski area? Ask yourself what you're looking for and use the information in this book to find it. I have tried to make *Ski Vermont!* the kind of book that will give you a look at Vermont's ski areas from a perspective you might not find elsewhere.

What's the best ski area in Vermont? If you really want to find out, start at the one nearest your home and ski your way around the state. It's a heck of a worthwhile piece of research, and by the end of winter you'll have the definitive answer. For you.

A note about prices: Because prices change from year to year, we have included none in this book. Instead, we have given relative price ranges, based on 1991 rates, designating areas as inexpensive, moderate, expensive or somewhere in between. Call the areas themselves for current rates. See Chapter 19 for some money-saving tips.

Chapter 1

Ascutney

Intermediate's Inspiration, Novice's Nirvana

D riving along Vermont's beautiful Interstate 91 near the Hartland Exit, have you ever wondered what that humungous mountain with the antennae sticking out of the top is? And, if you were driving south, did you notice a little white curl near the summit that looks as though it could be a ski trail?

What you've been looking at is Ascutney Mountain, the monadnock that towers above the rolling countryside of the Connecticut River valley. That curl of white is a ski trail, the easternmost loop of a trail network that faces north and looks down on the village of Brownsville and Route 44.

Now that you know what you're seeing, here's something else to consider: Ascutney Mountain is just the place to convince you that you're nearly ready for the next Winter Olympics. Like its neighbors, Pico and Okemo, Ascutney is an intermediate's inspiration, a novice's nirvana, a beginner's bliss.

Ascutney has some expert terrain (that curl is one of the steep sections of Old Ox Road) and a glade or two, but basically it plays to its strong suit — excellent intermediate skiing.

In the Abenaki language "ascutney" means "very steep slopes," and although relatively short by Vermont standards — the top of the Summit Chair is 2,250 feet above sea level — there are enough steep sections at Ascutney to stretch even advanced intermediates. The steeps are short because the mountain's vertical drop is a modest — again, by Vermont standards — 1,530 feet.

At first glance, 1,530 feet doesn't seem like a whole lot of mountain. Jay has 2,153; Sugarbush, 2,600. But vertical footage isn't crucial in determining how enjoyable (or even how steep) a mountain is. Snow King in Wyoming has only 1,500 vertical feet, and it's one of the steepest mountains in the country. More important than vertical footage are crowdedness and layout of the trails.

Crowdedness depends on lift capacity and popularity. Ascutney is not terribly strong in the uphill capacity department. It has four up-to-date chairlifts, but only one services the top of the mountain. So Ascutney has gone the other route, artificially controlling popularity by limiting ticket sales to 2,000 per day. This sales cap has meant that even on weekends and holidays liftlines are less than horrendous. Midweek, you can bounce on and off the lift like a yo-yo, getting in a full day's skiing in a few hours.

As for layout, Ascutney is a cruising hill, the sort that convinces intermediates that the Mahre brothers had better stay on their edges. Trails are wide without being I-91-wide. Grooming is so rigorous that most trails are as smooth as stair-runners of white shag carpet.

The pitch of Ascutney's trails is varied enough to keep them interesting and lively. Old Ox Road is a good example. Rated Most Difficult, it's really an intermediate trail with two steepish drops. Because of the meticulous grooming and the width of the trail, neither would give most mid-level skiers much trouble.

Two more ego-building trails are Broadway and Fifth Avenue, both of which come off the top and wend their way around the shoulder of the mountain before joining the broad slopes that lead to the base lodge. For more adventurous skiers, Upper Miller's Mile runs right under the chair, giving the opportunity for crowd-pleasing form and, when the moguls are up, even more crowd-pleasing wipeouts. Ascutney offers other niceties as well. One is a view from the top that takes in most of southern Vermont. Another is an elegant base lodge and even more elegant base hotel.

The lodge was built in 1963, then totally rebuilt in 1988, adding a second floor and refaced exterior to blend with the rest of the resort's handsome buildings. The hotel is one of those handsome buildings. It was completed in 1984 in that neo-Victorian style that in recent years has become the architectural style of choice at Vermont ski areas.

A third special feature of Ascutney is the Vermont Handicapped Ski and Sport Association. The area is the center for handicapped winter sports in the Northeast and has one of the most creative disabled skiing programs anywhere. Among its students are amputees, blind and deaf skiers, people with cerebral palsy and multiple sclerosis, and those with developmental disabilities. Ascutney's program includes individual instruction, ski clinics and NASTAR races. One of the pleasures of skiing there is to admire the progress of Ascutney's incredibly able disabled skiers who make the mountain their home hill.

Ascutney has 31 trails ranging from novice to expert, a friendly beginners' slope with its own chairlift, and 60 percent snowmaking coverage. Because of its relatively southern location and relatively low elevation, that snowmaking is important. Even with it, most expert trails require a good dump of natural snow to open. Fortunately, Ascutney's snowmakers and groomers are particularly good at what they do, and at times when ice is building up on nearby mountains, Ascutney often manages to create a soft, skiable surface.

Should you tire of skiing downhill, you can switch to skiing cross-country without leaving the area. At the foot of the mountain is the starting point for 32 kilometers of ski touring over rolling farms and through deciduous woods. The cross-country center has its own fully equipped rental shop.

Ascutney also has an outstanding sport and fitness center. It contains indoor and outdoor pools, seven tennis courts, racquetball, weights, saunas and massage. For families that include non-skiers, this can be a great aid in keeping everyone happy during a five-day ski week. The area's numerous condominiums are designed to blend in rather than dominate the scenery, and they are mercifully not located along the sides of ski trails above the beginner's area.

The Ascutney Mountain Resort Hotel has individual rooms and suites that come equipped with full kitchens and working fireplaces. Rooms and suites are handsomely appointed with colonial-style furniture. Dinners at the hotel's restaurant, the Ascutney Harvest Inn, are expensive and delicious. Other attractive nearby restaurants are Windsor Station in Windsor, Skunk Hollow Tavern in Hartland, Chase House in Cornish, New Hampshire, and the Home Hill Country Inn in Plainfield, New Hampshire. For off-slope lodging try the Mill Brook Bed and Breakfast in Brownsville and the Juniper Hill Inn in Windsor, the birthplace of Vermont.

The history of skiing on Ascutney Mountain goes back to 1938 when artist Bob Ely, a veteran of World War II's skiing Tenth Mountain Division, set up a 900-foot slope near the bottom of the hill. Later, Ascutney became a snowmaking pioneer, installing its first system in 1957. By then it had four rope tows and a T-bar dragging and pushing skiers uphill. In the 1960s a couple of chairlifts were added, along with two new T-bars.

But management changed. By the late 1970s the area's snowmaking

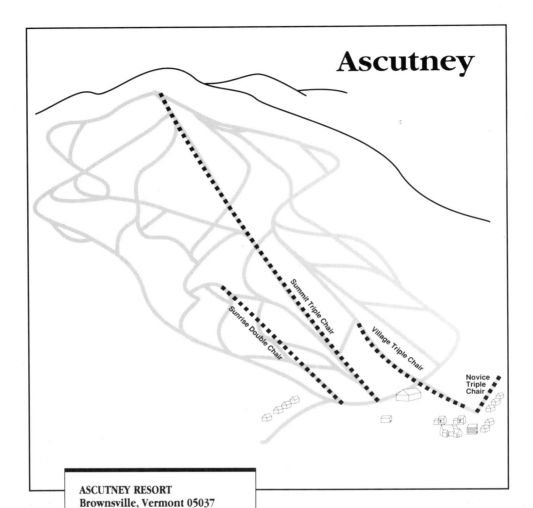

Ascutney

ASCUTNEY RESORT
Brownsville, Vermont 05037
(802) 484-7711 and (800) 243-0011
Base elevation: 720 feet
Top elevation: 2,250 feet
Vertical drop: 1,530 feet
Size: 100 acres of trails
Longest run: 2.5 miles
Terrain: Beginner 35%
Terrain: Intermediate 40%
Terrain: Advanced 25%
Snowmaking capacity: 60% of
  skiable terrain

had fallen by the wayside, and its lifts were begging for repair or replacement. The inevitable followed — gradual decline leading down the ever-more-slippery financial slopes. Bankruptcy was declared in March, 1983.

But in May of that year, a partnership of investors calling themselves Summit Ventures Inc.

bought the area. By November they had paid off the debts and managed to slap a coat of paint on the base lodge. That winter they drew only 12,000 skiers.

As the season wore on, the partners offered fervent prayers that the lift would keep running as long as the snow held out.

They nearly made it. Not until March did the main lift break down for good. They immediately declared the season over, then began ripping out cables and lift towers and pouring money into new lifts, snowmaking, condos, base lodge, hotel fitness center — the works. Their rescue efforts paid off. The moribund area was transformed into a thriving resort.

But the good times ended in 1990. This time a falling real estate market brought on the crash and return to bankruptcy. By the summer of 1991, the area was closed, at least temporarily, and its operation in the 1991–92 ski season was in doubt.

· · · · · · · · · · · · · · · · · · · ·

ASCUTNEY MOUNTAIN RESORT is a medium-priced, midsized mountain that is especially good for beginner and intermediate skiers and has attractive amenities and an outstanding program for disabled skiers.

KIDS: Ascutney offers four programs for children. Day care is for kids from six weeks to 10 years. The Teddy Bear Program introduces skiing to beginners from 3 to 5 years. The Polar Bear Program is for Teddy Bear graduates; Polar Bears ride the lifts; Teddy Bears don't. Finally, there's the SKIwee Program for 5- to 12-year-olds. It's instructional fun and games on snow. SKIwee is a national instruction program that gives out standardized report cards to kids. That way, if they spend a week this year at Ascutney and next year go to Okemo, they won't have to start all over or face being put in the wrong class.

TIP: Ski midweek — you can't beat it for wide open trails, no lift lines, smaller ski school groups, and individual attention.

WHERE: Ascutney is on Route 44 in Brownsville, in eastern Vermont near Windsor, seven miles from Exit 8 off Interstate 91.

Chapter 2

Bolton Valley

A Snowy Spot Families Love

Nineteen sixty-four was the year the state of Vermont bought the farm.

The farm in question was owned by Roland DesLauriers; the state needed it to build the Interstate 89 interchange in South Burlington. With the proceeds from the sale of his well-located 11 acres, DesLauriers bought a tract of 8,000 acres of mountainous logging land further down the new highway. The farm is now Howard Johnson's, the Sheraton, Holiday Inn and a pair of cloverleafs; the mountain is Bolton Valley Resort.

Interstate 89 and Bolton Valley are still tied together. It is I-89 — perhaps the most beautiful highway in the interstate system — that carries skiers to the town of Bolton, a town chartered by King George III in 1763. Reaching the ski area is a different story. The 4.2-mile access road is steep and winding; after a big snowfall, negotiating it requires good driving skills and good tread on the tires.

The steep ascent brings you to the ski resort with the highest base elevation in Vermont — 2,150 feet above sea level. That makes the climb doubly worthwhile. First, the high base elevation means a prolonged ski season, with snow holding over the whole mountain, not just the top 500 yards. Second, there is something delightful about the feel of a high-altitude alpine village that cannot be matched in the lowlands.

That alpine village atmosphere is just what Roland DesLauriers' son, Ralph, aimed for on his father's logging land. Before the end of 1964 he'd invested his life savings of $10,000 and persuaded two Vermont banks to ante up a million more to develop Bolton Valley Resort.

It worked. When you at last reach the top of the access road, your first impression is of having been transported to a Swiss village — even better, to a Swiss village without the cute Swiss filigrees that look so attractive in Switzerland and so ridiculous everywhere else.

Bolton Valley's architecture is sort of Universal Alpine — lots of wood and stucco, the ubiquitous clock tower, pretty gardens in summer, deep snowdrifts in winter. Thanks to its elevation, the resort village is cut off from the world. The awareness that I-89 is less than five miles down the road, and Burlington — Vermont's largest city — less than a half hour away quickly dims in the silence and beauty.

A midsize mountain, Bolton has a surprising diversity of trails. The most westerly (and most beautiful) is Peggy Dow's, originally Peggy Dow's Hymnal. A history buff, Ralph DesLauriers tends to give his trails names of historical significance; Peggy Dow was the wife of a pioneer Vermont preacher known for his vigorous sermonizing. The trail that bears her name is more sweet than vigorous; its only pungency comes from the smell of the balsam trees that line its sides. Stop and look through those trees and you'll see Lake Champlain and the Adirondack Mountains of New York State.

You get to Peggy Dow's from Chairlift I. Once you're in the chair, you know you're in safe hands. With the exception of the short Outlaw trail, every way down from the top is designed for intermediates or beginners. If you're looking for more challenge, take Lift IV, which starts halfway up the mountain. Hard Luck, Spillway and Show Off are all sharply pitched and just long enough to work up a sweat. Not only does the well-named Show Off run directly under the lift, but it has a king-sized boulder left in the trail that launches young daredevils to frightening heights. (They're particularly frightening for unwary chairlift riders who find themselves in the flight path of young men hurtling through space, apparently aimed directly at them. However, as in Disney World, the hurtling figure drops away before contact is made.)

Bolton's newest lift, the quadruple chair, services Timberline, a high-intermediate area whose trails connect with the other lifts. Timberline has its own base area and parking lot below the other lifts and the village.

The village is at the heart of the Bolton Valley experience. The layout of Bolton's amenities has been carefully planned so that everything is within a few minutes walk of everything else. Once the car is parked, it stays parked until it's time to go home. The three main-mountain lifts are just up from the hotel. The impressive health center, complete with indoor pool and four tennis courts, is just down from the hotel. There

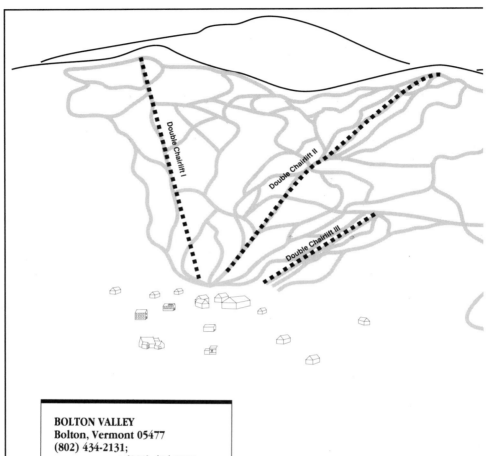

BOLTON VALLEY
Bolton, Vermont 05477
(802) 434-2131;
  snow report (802) 434-2131
  and (800) 451-3220 (in
  New England, outside Vermont)
Base elevation: 1,525 feet
Top elevation: 3,150 feet
Vertical drop: 1,625 feet
Size: 140 acres of trails
Longest run: 2.5 miles
Terrain: Beginner 28%
Terrain: Intermediate 49%
Terrain: Advanced 23%
Annual snowfall: 250 inches
Snowmaking capacity: 60% of
  skiable terrain

are eight restaurants scattered in and around the village. They're all a walk from the room, not a ride.

Of course, walking isn't every-

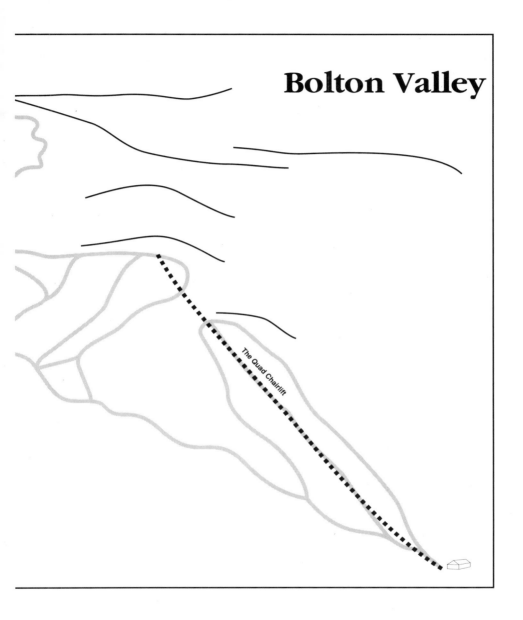

Bolton Valley

The Quad Chairlift

one's idea of a good time. For Los Angelinos and others who don't feel quite comfortable unless they put in at least a few miles behind the wheel each day, Bolton is ideally situated.

To the west lies Burlington, a city with considerable charm, a great array of eateries and drinkeries, a trafficless shopping mall on the main street and an abundance of cultural events. The culture is thanks to the University of Vermont's Lane Series, and other local impresarios, and from having four colleges within whistling distance of one another. For music, drama and sporting events, you'd be hard-pressed to find another small American city with such a wealth of choices.

Between Bolton and Montpelier is Waterbury, a little town known especially for some nearby businesses: Cold Hollow Cider Mill in Waterbury Center and the Ben and Jerry's ice-cream factory just north of the I-89 exit. Both are among the state's top year-round attractions, both make the finest of Vermont products, and both let visitors watch them do it. If you like chocolate, don't miss the rich offerings of the Green Mountain Chocolate Company on Route 100 in Duxbury.

Side-trips to places like these are great midweek breaks for the family on a long skiing vacation. Another kind of break is cross-country skiing. Bolton Valley has over 100 kilometers of Nordic trails and a cross-country center that rents skis and serves free popcorn by the old pot-bellied stove. Because its trails range between 2,000 and 3,000 feet, they are among the first in Vermont to open and the last to close.

Bolton prides itself on its family orientation. Its small village atmosphere gives parents the feeling their kids are safe even when out of sight. And absence of automobile traffic means one less hazard parents have to worry about on vacation.

Expansion has increased the Timberline quad chair's capacity by 60 percent, opened a whole new mountain, and increased the drop to 1,600 vertical feet. In addition to the new quad, Bolton has four vintage double chairs and, for beginners, a surface lift. Because lift capacity exceeds bed capacity, even on sunny weekends when large numbers of Burlingtonians drop in for a day on the slopes lift lines at Bolton rarely exceed 15 minutes. Most weekdays, they're non-existent.

Bolton Valley is a member of Ski Vermont's Classics, which sells an interchangeable lift pass good at Jay Peak, Mad River Glen, Sugarbush, Stowe and Smuggler's Notch. Bolton also offers something unavailable at any other major Vermont resort — night skiing. Genuine ski fanatics drive up to the mountain early enough to be first on the lift, ski all morning, wolf down a sandwich on the Timberline quad, ski all afternoon, grab a quick dinner, then ski under the lights. Night skiing is from 4 to 10 p.m. every night except Sunday. You can ski from 9 in the morning until 10 at night or until you collapse, whichever comes first. Dress warmly.

Bolton's new lodge is bright, airy and full of delightful touches — fresh flowers in the lobby, handmade quilts on the beds. The old lodge is Spartan by comparison, but it's getting a facelift. The resort's eateries have been undergoing their own lift. Lindsay's is an elegant dining room, the Cafe Cortina a checkered-table-clothed casual Italian bistro. The Fireside serves everything from a taco salad to a steak dinner all day and until 9:30 at night.

After-dinner nightlife at Bolton is limited to what's on the mountain. The drinking spots are the Cortina, Lindsay's bar and the James Moore Tavern. Fortunately, the James Moore books just the right sort of talent for most skiers — danceable music loud enough to get tired feet tapping but not so loud as to render conversation impossible. For teens and others looking for an alcohol-free evening, the Sports Center shows movies every two hours and offers pool (swimming and table varieties), Ping-Pong, tennis, volleyball and video games. And those poor souls caught in the clutches of ski fever can just keep skiing until the lights go out.

. . . .

BOLTON VALLEY is a well-groomed mountain that catches a lot of snow. It's a resort village designed for families having fun together yet it's intimate enough for couples sneaking off to a romantic getaway. Bolton is mid-range in size, price and difficulty. It's the closest mountain to the Burlington International Airport and the only one for miles that lets you ski after the sun goes down.

TIP: When the middle of the mountain gets a little too crowded for your liking, try exploring the outer trails off Chairlift I and the Timberline area for some quiet, relaxed cruising terrain.

KIDS: Bolton has for many years run an exceptional children's program. It's divided into the Honeybear Nursery and two SKIwee-affiliated groups, the Bolton Bears and the Bolton Cubs. The Bears are aged 6 to 12; the Cubs, 5 to 7. The nursery, which takes children from 3 months to 6 years, runs a ski program for 4- to 5-year-olds. All guests' children who are 6 and under ski and sleep free. Bolton also has a Kids Night Out, an evening activity program for youngsters from 6 to 11.

WHERE: Bolton is off Route 2 in central Vermont between Burlington and Montpelier. Take Route 2 from the Waterbury or Richmond exits off Interstate 89. The access road is about eight miles from either exit.

Chapter 3
Bromley
Pampered, Sunny Slopes

Bromley and Magic Mountain are stepsisters. They share ownership and proximity but little else.

Magic is a twin-peaked baked Alaska; Bromley is big single scoop of vanilla ice cream. Magic's trails are backroads Vermont; Bromley's are more like the Champs-Elysées. Magic attracts swinging singles driving Porsches. Bromley skiers pile out of Volvo station wagons with Connecticut plates. Magic started in 1960. Bromley has always been there.

Or so it seems. Bromley is now in its sixth decade, which makes it an ancient among ski areas. The mountain is so steeped in ski history that it feels as though there's never been a time without a Big Bromley, sitting there east of Manchester in the town of Peru, facing Route 11, gathering snow at night and sunshine in the day.

It was opened in 1936 by Fred Pabst, an heir to the Pabst and Schlitz beer fortunes. Pabst did for skiing in the late 1930s and early 1940s what Mount Snow's Walter Schoenknecht was to do on a bigger scale in the mid-1950s — make it accessible to the masses, not just the superfit. Pabst's motto was "Pamper the people."

It was to this end that Bromley was manicuring its slopes when other mountains accepted boulders in the trail as part of nature's plan. It's why Bromley was building J-bars when other mountains were extending their rope tows. (The J-bar, Pabst's invention and source of greatest pride, was essentially a T-bar with one side missing.) It's why Bromley opened one of the first ski nurseries, practically invented wide teaching slopes and was making snow when others were merely praying for it.

Besides the innovations that worked (the J-bar worked; it just didn't last), Pabst had a major one that failed completely. In the 1930s he tried a chain-store approach to running ski areas. At one point he owned areas in Vermont, Quebec, New Hampshire, New York, Wisconsin — anywhere he could find a hill near a railway station, Fred Pabst installed a tow and started selling tickets.

But it didn't work. There weren't enough skiers, and little of the money generated at these far-flung outposts found its way back to the parent company. So, in 1941 he disposed of all but one. The one he kept was Big Bromley.

Pabst had purchased Bromley for roughly $10 an acre, and had immediately begun grooming it. To Pabst, grooming was serious business. He dynamited, bulldozed, graded, raked, fertilized and sowed countless bags of grass seed. In the end he had what he wanted — a mountain that could be skied and skied well on just four inches of snow. While it attracted skiers of all abilities, Bromley had the lock on beginners and intermediates. The combination of wide beginners' slopes, a dedicated ski school, child care facilities, a sun-warmed southern exposure, early snowmaking and that legendary grooming made for a kind of skiing that just wasn't available elsewhere.

Today, most of Bromley's — the "Big" in "Big Bromley" was dropped some years ago — 161 skiable acres are best suited for beginning and intermediate skiers. With the exception of the liftlines, Upper Twister and Sunder, the entire South Face is graded Easiest and More Difficult.

But not all of the mountain is quite so tame. The East Side is mogul country. Serviced by the Blue Ribbon quad, a chairlift installed at the end of 1988, trails like Pabst Panic, Havoc and Avalanche have a little more kick. All are rated Most Difficult, and all have 100 percent snowmaking capacity.

The tradition of pampering the people remains alive today. With its heavy commitment to snowmaking, even when the relatively light (150 inches a year) snowfall and south-facing slopes combine to limit natural cover, the odds are good that conditions will be fine at Bromley.

With the recent addition of the Blue Ribbon quad, Bromley now has seven chairlifts and two surface lifts. If you're heading for the top, it matters little which one you take since most end up within a few yards of each other just below the peak. The longest and oldest is the Number One Chair, which begins its measured ascent just below the base lodge. The shortest is the Learning Center Lift, a cable tow with plastic handles that hauls first-time skiers up Bromley's short and reassuring learner's area.

Although the Bromley motto is "Very Vermont," its skiing more typifies Canada's Laurentians than the Green Mountains. A round-topped mountain, wide trails fanning out from a single summit, the ambiance of a large, (though unusually well-mannered) family, and nothing scary unless you go looking for it — Bromley has the feel of an English-speaking Quebec area.

Like the Laurentians, there's a certain similarity about most of Brom-

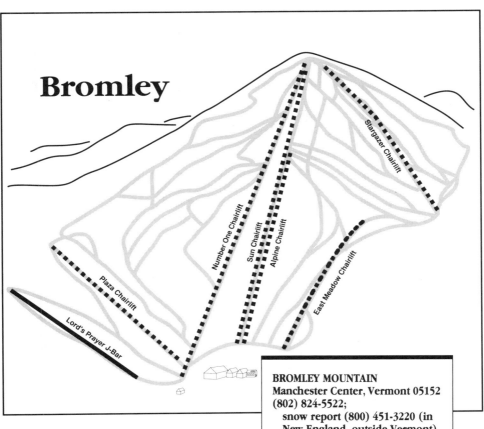

Bromley

Number One Chairlift
Sun Chairlift
Alpine Chairlift
Stargazer Chairlift
East Meadow Chairlift
Plaza Chairlift
Lord's Prayer J-Bar

BROMLEY MOUNTAIN
Manchester Center, Vermont 05152
(802) 824-5522;
  snow report (800) 451-3220 (in
  New England, outside Vermont)
Base elevation: 1,950 feet
Top elevation: 3,150 feet
Vertical drop: 1,625 feet
Size: 161 acres of trails
Longest run: 2.5 miles
Terrain: Beginner 35%
Terrain: Intermediate 34%
Terrain: Advanced 31%
Annual snowfall: 150 inches
Snowmaking capacity: 83% of
  skiable terrain

ley's South Face trails. The longest run on the hill is Run Around/Upper Thruway/Lower Thruway, an easy 2.5-mile ramble down the western edge of the South Face. Upper and Lower Twister run straight down the liftline, and East Meadow is a gradual, pasture-wide descent from mid-station on the Alpine chairlift.

Bromley's snow groomers like to leave a few powder runs and, on the East Side, mogul trails. This brings welcome variety to a somewhat homogeneous trail system.

Skiers who want to stay on the mountain either book a condo — and these are the original slopeside condos in the East — at Bromley Village, (802) 824-5458, or stay at the privately owned Bromley Sun Lodge, within walking distance of the lifts. If you are staying nearby, consider bringing your own lunch — Bromley's cafeteria is, at least on weekends, crowded beyond its capacity. Fortunately there's plenty of satisfying dining within a few miles of the area.

Bargain hunters will appreciate two Bromley policies. The first is a shared ticket with its stepsister, Magic Mountain. The second is that early risers ski free from 8:30 to 9 a.m. on weekends, 9–9:30 on weekdays.

. . . .

BROMLEY is a historic, sunny, largely beginner and intermediate mountain whose strongest features include the ski school, snowmaking, and warmth. Prices are moderate, midweek prices are a bargain. It's long been a favorite for family skiing and sun worshipping.

TIP: Try the Beginner's Circle package. It's a continuous teaching program for beginners and those who have not skied in a long time. You learn at your own pace and take breaks whenever you want.

KIDS: Bromley's long-established children's programs cater to youngsters from 6 to 12 years. Three- to 5-year-olds join the Mighty Moose Club or Beginner Discoverski. Six- to 14-year-olds go to Discoverski School. The Bromley Nursery watches over pre-skiers from one month to 6 years.

WHERE: Bromley is on Route 11, six miles east of Manchester in southwestern Vermont.

Chapter 4

Burke Mountain

Skiing as It Used to Be

Burke Mountain has long been the smart skier's best-kept secret. Remote, rustic, old-fashioned — the area is a genuine throwback. Skiing Burke is like skiing half the mountains in Vermont, circa 1960.

Everyone knows everyone else. Staff and skiers talk to each other more like neighbors meeting at the post office than employees and guests. There's only one lift to the summit, and except on occasional weekends, lift lines are what's goin' on down-country, not here.

Given the fact that all these old-fashioned virtues are part of a beautiful and eminently skiable mountain, Burke is a secret well worth keeping.

However, much of Burke's anachronistic existence has been the result of laid-back management style, limited finances and lack of available lodging. The area's low-budget operation long restricted advertising to a fraction of its competitors', and if, by chance, large numbers of skiers did descend on the mountain, there was no place to house and feed them.

But minimal management was only part of the reason for Burke's reclusive existence. The rest can be summed up in three words: location, location, location.

Even more than Jay Peak, Burke stands alone. It is by far the easternmost ski area in Vermont, located northeast of the Lyndonville exit on Interstate 91. That places it in the midst of the Northeast Kingdom and means the mountain is surrounded by abundant natural beauty and very little else. A region that considers St. Johnsbury a major metropolis isn't exactly a high-density population center. What's more, to get to Burke from Boston, New York, or Montreal, you have to pass half the ski mountains in New Hampshire, Vermont or Eastern Canada.

Small and remote may be beautiful, but it has twice driven Burke Mountain into bankruptcy court. Burke's been down — indisputably down — but it isn't out. Although currently owned by a creditor bank, it has been infused with new amenities.

The old double chair has been replaced with a quad. The base lodge has been upgraded. Even Burke's vow of silence has been broken — the area now reminds Hartford residents they are but four hours, Bostonians they are but three hours, and Montrealers they are a mere two-and-a-half hours from "Vermont's Sweet Spot," and they don't even have to get off the Interstate until they hit Exit 23 in Lyndonville. In short, Burke is doing the unforgivable — telling the world about Vermont's secret mountain.

That mountain is a serious skier's dream. With 2,000 feet of vertical

drop (1,750 feet for the skier above novice level), Burke offers surprising variety, terrifying steeps, some of the best old-fashioned narrow-trail skiing in the state, and a wonderful beginner's area. (That's the other 250 vertical feet.)

Skiing Burke reminds you how beautiful skiing can be. Trails cut through the woods offer protection from cold north winds. Finding yourself alone beside a stand of frost-covered maples or in the midst of a dense forest of snow-laden spruce recalls the throat-catching beauty of old-fashioned skiing. Hitting Burke on a weekday and discovering you have the whole mountain to yourself is nothing short of a fantasy come true.

But before you step into your bindings, remember that Burke is a northern mountain and tends to label its trails differently from many of its southern cousins. What's marked Easiest here would be More Difficult farther south. What's marked More Difficult would rate a Most Difficult black diamond at Okemo.

Burke has one Easiest trail, Toll Road, coming off its 3,267-foot summit. It's the mountain's longest and best-loved beginner's trail. A sharply inclined, hairpin-turned drive in summer, when covered with snow it becomes a winding ramble through the trees. Toll Road is a lovely place to learn to ski, with winding turns, moderate steepness and never a dull stretch.

Toll Road is a good place to start the day, but for intermediates and up, East Bowl is even better. On relatively busy days, it's often deserted — because East Bowl is easily missed. To get there, turn left at the top of the Willoughby quad chair, then angle right onto an unmarked path over a hillock. It means a little climbing, but that, too, is an honorable part of skiing. The trail meanders down the east side of the mountain, giving solitude, spectacular views — those massive mountains to the east are the Presidential Range in New Hampshire — and enough pitch and narrowness to make a beginner's heart skip. It also has enough uphill at the beginning and end to keep those same hearts pumping. With all that skating and poling required to get back to the lift, East Bowl is the ideal warm-up trail.

Doug's Drop will keep your heart pumping, too, but for different reasons. Narrow, steep and often deeply drifted, it keeps experts on their toes — or puts them on their bottoms. Bear Den/Ledges is just as challenging and should be avoided except when there's a lot of snow cover. On snow-lean days those ledges are death on P-tex.

To the right of the chair, Upper and Lower Willoughby are fast intermediate runs that turn to expert when heavy with new snow. Fox's Folly is a long, straight chute right under the chair. It's a trail just made for daredevils.

Speaking of daredevils, those incredibly fast young skiers who keep whizzing by you at Burke are either a ski team — teams from as far away as New Zealand have trained on the mountain — or students at Burke Mountain Academy. The academy, which is within easy reach of the base lodge, is one of the premier ski racing schools in America. Incidentally, those teams often favor the 1955 Mountain Poma lift rather than the 1989 chairlift. And because the beginners' area has its own chairlift, novices need not fear being blasted off the mountain by a blur of racers bearing down on them at the speed of sound.

The beginners' terrain is on the lower mountain under the Sherburne Farm double chair. It's a fine place for new skiers because its trails combine easy incline with considerable length. Dashney Mile, Sherman's March, Bunker Hill and Carter Country offer the novice a chance to practice linking turns, secure in the knowledge that nothing steeper than a bowling alley is around the next bend.

Burke has made major dents in two perennial problems — and has one to go. The new quad chairlift, installed on the pylons of the old double, has doubled the mountain's uphill capacity. New condos built around the beginners' slope have helped ease the chronic shortage of rooms (though at the price of diminishing the wild beauty of the area). The major remaining problem is lack of snowmaking. Only Willoughby has snow guns from top to bottom, and the majority of trails still depend on nature for their cover. Solving the lift and room problems has taken

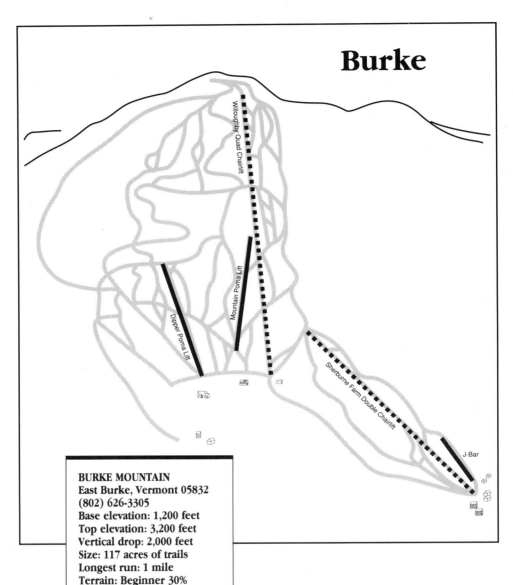

Burke

Willoughby Quad Chairlift

Mountain Poma Lift

Diaper Poma Lift

Sherburne Farm Double Chairlift

J-Bar

BURKE MOUNTAIN
East Burke, Vermont 05832
(802) 626-3305
Base elevation: 1,200 feet
Top elevation: 3,200 feet
Vertical drop: 2,000 feet
Size: 117 acres of trails
Longest run: 1 mile
Terrain: Beginner 30%
Terrain: Intermediate 40%
Terrain: Advanced 30%
Annual snowfall: 170 inches
Snowmaking capacity: 25% of
   skiable terrain

a major injection of cash. It will take a further financial commitment to make snow in sufficient quantity to get the mountain through those inevitable winters when bountiful nature goes on an austerity budget.

What do you do at Burke after the lifts close? If you're looking for wild times, you'll probably have to drive 'til you hit Stowe or Sugarbush. If you're looking for quiet times, stick around.

In addition to Burke Mountain's own Vertical Drop Restaurant and Lounge, which serves light dinners, the area boasts some interesting restaurants within easy driving distance. The closest is the Old Cutter Inn, half a mile from the mountain and adjacent to Burke Mountain's highly regarded cross-country trail system. The Old Cutter has charming rooms and serves excellent continental dinners in a beautiful setting.

Along the shores of Lake Willoughby in Westmore is the rebuilt Willoughvale Inn. The owners have gone to considerable expense to make it an attractive place to stay and a memorable place to eat.

Farther afield, between Burke Mountain and Jay Peak, is Heermansmith Farm Inn, which combines lovely old-fashioned rooms, an antique-filled dining room and miles of groomed cross-country ski terrain. Down in St. Johnsbury, Tucci's mixes kitsch-Italian decor, excellent Italian cuisine and the most creative doggie-bags in the state.

OK, after the lifts have closed and you've had your meal, what do you do at Burke? There's the Pub Outback for rousing and carousing, Bailey's Country Store for stopping and shopping, and with a little luck, you could hit something special in Lyndonville or St. Johnsbury. The special something is Catamount Arts, which presents exotic films and varied theater. You can call to find out what's on: (802) 748-2600.

If you're not staying at one of the mountain condos, try one of the local inns: the Wildflower, Garrison, Nutmegger, Sprucewood or Hansel & Gretel Haus.

• • • • • • • • • • • • • • • • • • •

BURKE MOUNTAIN is an uncrowded, low-priced, medium-sized mountain in the heart of the Northeast Kingdom with a great variety of terrain and gorgeous scenery.

TIP: Try some of the lesser known trails like McHarg's Cut-off and you may discover some light, fluffy powder that no one else has yet found.

KIDS: Burke's day care area accommodates kids from 3 months to 5 years. Its SKIwee program teaches skiing to those 4 years and up. There's also lollipop races, snow play and a serious race training program for kids who like to go fast and are at least 7.

WHERE: Burke Mountain is in northeastern Vermont, near St. Johnsbury and Lyndonville. Take exit 23 or 24 off Interstate 91, and follow Route 114 to East Burke. It's seven miles from Interstate to mountain.

Chapter 5
Haystack Mountain
A Gentle, Sunny and Southern Spot

The story of Haystack Mountain is a tale of death and resurrection.

As Vermont's second-southernmost, then southernmost mountain (it moved to first place when Hogback Mountain closed in 1985), Haystack seemed like a can't-fail proposition. It was, after all, closer to the major population centers of Connecticut than to Burlington, had a reasonable elevation (3,200 feet), a respectable-if-not-spectacular vertical drop (1,400 feet), and a sunny position. How could it go wrong?

It managed. In the early 1970s, Haystack embarked on an ambitious and expensive program of expansion. Among the big-ticket items were a cluster-housing development and an 18-hole golf course. The expansion coincided perfectly with:

- *a national recession,*
- *a steep increase in interest rates,*
- *a nationwide gasoline shortage and, as if that weren't enough,*
- *a couple of nearly snowless winters.*

The mountain went into receivership.

Then the receiver went into receivership.

The chairlifts stopped. Rust took over the machinery. Maple saplings took over the trails. Pine trees took over the golf course sand traps. Unlike Burke Mountain, which managed to keep running through its Chapter Eleven years, Haystack died. Those who had bought a vacation home with a view of the golf course merely felt like dying.

But in 1982, at another Vermont mountain, a management change was under way that would have a major impact on Haystack's future. Don Tarinelli left his job as president of Stratton Mountain Corporation, taking a fair number of his staff with him. Tarinelli formed the Haystack Group Incorporated, which promptly bought Haystack's non-operational operation, lock, stock and rusting chairlifts. The deal was completed in 1984.

By 1985 the Haystack Group had managed to invest $3 million in the ultra-high-risk undertaking of bringing a dead ski resort back to life. Its first purchase was a sorely needed snowmaking system. Next came three new triple chairlifts. The golf course, which had lain fallow for nine years, was hayed, and its sand traps stripped of trees and brush. New condos were built, as well as a new base lodge. By the end of the resurrection, the investment ran close to $14 million.

And just when it began to look like the investment might pay off, along came the end of the 1980s. In 1990 the real estate boom imploded, and Haystack's investors once again found themselves attempting to bail out a sinking enterprise. The mountain is (as of this writing) in full operation, and the skiing's fine; it's just that there isn't a lot of money in the kitty. It's all been spent on the mountain.

What are the results of all that spending? Take a tour of the area, starting with the new facilities. Begin with the ultra-modern base lodge, walk down to the attractive housing clusters just below it, then move up to the three late-model chairlifts. Everything looks freshly minted and squeaky clean.

Now check out the terrain. Again, walk down from the base lodge, this time stopping at the beginner's area. It has its own lifts, its own slopes and its own low-priced ticket. No daredevils will ruin your day here; this is the exclusive territory of learners trying to master the wedge turn and the vertical stop.

Next, hike back to the lodge and look out its massive front windows. Above and directly in front of you is the main mountain. Over to the left is the Witches, Haystack's expert area. While the trails aren't long enough to burn your thighs, they're steep enough to churn your stomach. Gandolf, Cauldron and Merlin are those rapid drops on the extreme left of the hill. By the time you get to Wizard, the pitch is a bit more forgiving. Working your way over to Spellbinder and Shadow (which lead back to the main mountain), you'll be comfortable even if you're an intermediate skier.

On the main hill, everything except Stump Jumper can be handled by intermediates, and the majority of trails are within the grasp of advanced beginners. The most beautiful trail — and also the longest — is Last Chance/Outcast, which meanders around the far side of Haystack Mountain before circling back to the base lodge. The bit of trail network you can see from the top is the Carinthia section of nearby Mount Snow.

These slopes are ideal for learners, intermediates and families of differing abilities. All trails lead back to the lodge, and the warm southern (well, southern Vermont) sun keeps everybody happy.

Haystack's gentle contours probably wouldn't do much for a racing

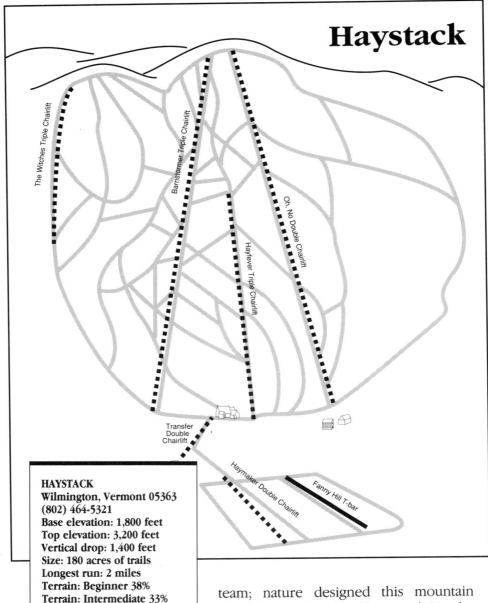

Haystack

The Witches Triple Chairlift

Barnstormer Triple Chairlift

Oh, No Double Chairlift

Hayfever Triple Chairlift

Transfer
Double
Chairlift

Haymaker Double Chairlift

Fanny Hill T-bar

HAYSTACK
Wilmington, Vermont 05363
(802) 464-5321
Base elevation: 1,800 feet
Top elevation: 3,200 feet
Vertical drop: 1,400 feet
Size: 180 acres of trails
Longest run: 2 miles
Terrain: Beginner 38%
Terrain: Intermediate 33%
Terrain: Advanced 29%
Annual snowfall: 120 inches
Snowmaking capacity: 90% of
skiable terrain

team; nature designed this mountain more for comfort than for speed. But the mountain is a growing favorite with snowboarders, who like its wide trails and forgiving terrain.

When you've finished skiing, you can have a drink in the base lodge and listen to the local musical talent. Or, you can head out for something to eat. Since Haystack and Mount Snow are so close, local restaurants and night spots have been divided between the two chapters. Check them both.

For breakfast, try Dot's, just down the road — a lot of the locals do. Deerfield's serves pizza, pasta and ribs, the Old Red Mill has an unusually good salad bar, the Red Anchor specializes in — you guessed it — fresh seafood, and there are a dozen other moderately priced eating choices in the region. For top-of-the-line dining, make a reservation at the Hermitage, Red Shutters or Le Petit Chef. The Roadhouse is a highly regarded steak house with modest prices.

Here's a suggestion for ski schoolers: Haystack ski school now offers SyberVision, a neuro-muscular video aid. At the beginning of each lesson students watch a 10-minute video featuring expert skiers performing basic maneuvers. As the tape runs in slow motion, light accentuates the ankles, knees, hips and shoulders of the experts. The purpose is to imprint in the students a memory of perfect technique before they head for the slopes to complete their lesson with qualified instructors. And most people who try it say it actually works.

• • • • • • • • • • • • • • • • • • •

HAYSTACK MOUNTAIN is a sweet, sunny, southern ski area with modern facilities and a friendly style. It's moderately expensive on weekends, a great bargain midweek and for beginners.

TIP: If you're skiing further north, stop at Haystack on Sunday morning and ski until 1 p.m. for a reduced price.

KIDS: Day care is available for kids from 2 through 7, half or full days. The children's ski school teaches 3- to 11-year-olds, also half or full day. Both programs serve lunch for their full-day sessions.

WHERE: Haystack is off Route 100 north of Wilmington in southern Vermont. Turn left on Colebrook Road, it's two miles to the access road.

Chapter 6

Jay Peak

A Big Mountain with a Quebec Flavor

When you're skiing Jay, you're skiing north.

You begin to grasp just how far north when you stop near the top of Northway, just under the tram station, and try to figure out what that nearby ski area is and why it doesn't appear on your Vermont map.

The area is Owl's Head, and it's in Canada. If you continued down Northway and somehow found a trail through the woods, you'd be in Canada, too. *"Bonjour. Bienvenue.* Are you carrying any liquor or firearms?"

Not only is Jay Peak the northernmost ski area in Vermont, for years it was also the most notorious. It gained its notoriety from wildly optimistic snow reports, poorly groomed trails and snarling employees. If that weren't enough, in a display of astonishing cultural insensitivity, the Austrian drill sergeants who taught at the ski school used to end every lesson by insisting that their perplexed-looking classes shout, "Heil, ski!"

When the current management — four Montreal businessmen and American Bill Stenger — bought the area in 1978, they found a demoralized staff, rundown equipment and an unenviable local reputation.

Led by Stenger, now the resort's president and general manager, the new owners turned all that around in a remarkably short time. Jay Peak is one of the few operations of any kind that has become bigger and friendlier, more successful and more personable, and increasingly profitable at the same time.

As the northern outpost of Vermont skiing, Jay stands alone, overlooking Lake Memphremagog to the east, Lake Champlain to the west, northern Vermont to the south, and what looks like most of Canada to the north.

The view is stunning. Some days you stand on the peak — Jay has a real peak, not a broad plateau at the top — and look down on clouds trapped between the smaller peaks below, then over the sweep of the great plains of Quebec, and all you can do is shake your head in silent wonder.

The Quebec influence is strong here, stronger than at any other

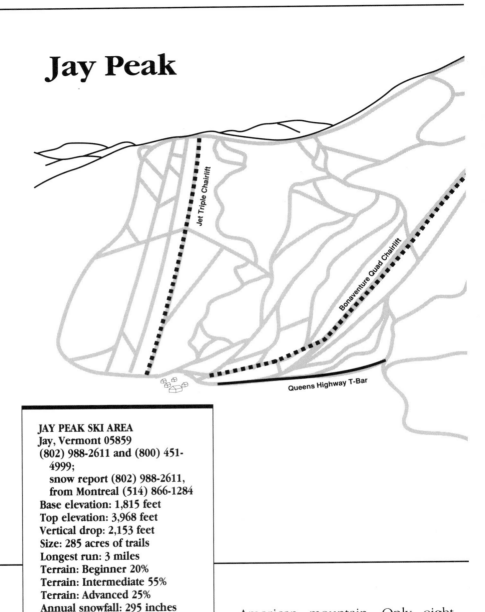

Jay Peak

Jet Triple Chairlift

Bonaventure Quad Chairlift

Queens Highway T-Bar

JAY PEAK SKI AREA
Jay, Vermont 05859
(802) 988-2611 and (800) 451-
4999;
   snow report (802) 988-2611,
   from Montreal (514) 866-1284
Base elevation: 1,815 feet
Top elevation: 3,968 feet
Vertical drop: 2,153 feet
Size: 285 acres of trails
Longest run: 3 miles
Terrain: Beginner 20%
Terrain: Intermediate 55%
Terrain: Advanced 25%
Annual snowfall: 295 inches
Snowmaking capacity: 80% of
   skiable terrain

American mountain. Only eight miles from the border, Jay's atmosphere owes a lot to the Quebecois. On an average weekend, in winter

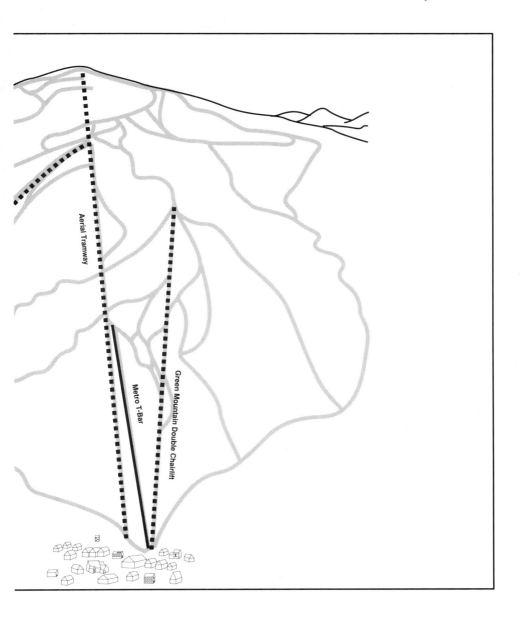

Aerial Tramway

Metro T-Bar

Green Mountain Double Chairlift

or any other season (Jay's tram, the only one in Vermont, hauls visitors to the peak year 'round), more people are speaking French than English. The stylishness that characterizes Montrealers makes the Jay cafeteria the best-dressed eatery south of the border. For those seeking culture while learning to parallel, some of Jay's ski classes are conducted in French. This is Vermont's bicultural, bilingual ski resort.

It is also a skier's ski resort. With an elevation of nearly 4,000 feet, a 2,153-foot vertical drop and 50 miles of trails, Jay has always attracted heavy-duty skiers. Stateside is a self-contained, all-expert area, and its liftline trail, the Jet, is steep, wide and mogully as an egg carton. What's worse (or better, depending on your bump ability and show-off quotient), every minute you're struggling to survive this tricky trail, you're in full view of the voluble commentators riding the lift and critiquing your technique in two languages.

For more reticent skiers looking for a steep and narrow trail with considerably more privacy, Kitzbuehel is the answer. Although the Jet is the new kind of expert trail — steep, wide and straight as a ski pole, Kitzbuehel is that increasingly rare old kind, a long series of narrow pitches that twist and turn down the side of the mountain.

While Jay's reputation as a hotshot's mountain is secure, in recent years it has made its biggest improvements in its beginner and intermediate areas. Today, 20 percent of its terrain is for inexperienced skiers, 55 percent for intermediates and 25 percent for experts. New skiers love Interstate and Harmony Lane, the two long, wide, gentle slopes serviced by the Metro T-bar. Intermediates prefer Green Mountain Boys and Racer, which come off the Green Mountain chairlift.

As for snow, Jay gets the biggest drop in Vermont, an average of 300 inches a year. Combined with constantly expanding snowmaking capability, this once icy mountain now has good snow most of the time.

The price paid for all these improvements is increased popularity, which translates to big weekend crowds through most of the winter. Here's how to beat the masses to the slopes. Take the 8:30 tram to the summit, then ski Vermonter to the triple chair. Ski the triple until 10:30 or when it starts getting busy. Then ski back to the tram side for an early lunch around 11. When the hordes hit the cafeteria at noon, you head back to the triple. At 1:30, when lunch hour ends, swing back to the tram and ski its trails for the rest of the day.

When planning an overnight trip to Jay Peak, you need to choose between three distinct geographical locations for bed and board.

One is on the mountain itself. Although Route 242, which crosses Jay from east to west, has digs of various style and price, the likely choice is right at the foot of the slopes in the Hotel Jay or at the solidly constructed, well-run condominiums that abut it. Just west of the ski area, the Inglenook Lodge is a full-service lodge with a great chef and the only indoor swimming pool in the region.

If you're not on the mountain, you'll need to go east, to Montgomery and vicinity, or west to Jay Village, Troy and North Troy. On the Montgomery side of the mountain, the Belfry is the local favorite for casual dining; the Black Lantern for something a bit more elegant. To the west, the Jay Village Inn offers clean, adequate rooms and consistently good food. For bed and breakfasts, Rose Apple Acres Farm in North Troy draws raves as does the Woodshed Lodge (winters only) which is closer to the mountain. For an outstanding breakfast and a reasonably priced room, the White Porch Inn (802-988-4048) is hard to beat. If you're in a condo and crave a special treat, Daria MonDesire, owner-baker of A Baker Named Desire, will create a knock-your-belt-off dessert you can feast on at home.

Another thing you should know about Jay Peak: along with Bolton Valley, Mad River Glen, Sugarbush, Stowe and Smugglers' Notch, Jay is a member of Ski Vermont's Classics. These resorts sell an interchangeable lift pass, good for three or five days out of seven. Passholders ski any or all of the mountains at less than the daily rate and without purchasing separate tickets.

What's not to like at Jay? When it's cold, it's really cold. And if you're looking for wild and crazy nightlife, you'll probably have to keep looking. The pseudo-Swiss A-frames and chalets that decorate the surrounding countryside look as out of place in Vermont as sugar maples in Miami.

· · · · · · · · · · · · · · · · · · ·

JAY PEAK has a huge mountain, a wide variety of terrain, unforgettable views and friendly service, from the lift attendants — perhaps the best lift attendants anywhere — to the general manager. All that and the Quebec flavor make Jay Peak an exciting, exotic place to ski. Jay is moderately priced on weekends, a great bargain for Vermonters midweek.

TIP: When Jay gets busy, try Ullr's Dream. It doesn't get the traffic that the other trails do, and it's the most scenic way down the mountain.

KIDS: For resort guests staying on the property, children stay free; kids under 6 ski free as well. Child care for children of guests is complimentary from 9 a.m. to 9 p.m., and there's a supervised children's hour as well. The SKIwee program offers lessons for 5- to 12-year-olds who already have skiing experience. Day care operates all day for children from 2 to 7 with indoor activities and skiing option.

WHERE: Jay Peak is in northwestern Vermont a few miles from the Canadian border. Follow Route 242 until you see signs for the ski area.

Chapter 7

Killington

The Mountain with More of Everything

This is going to be hard to believe:

There was a time when Killington was just another ski area. A largish mountain, a couple of Poma lifts, nice views. When it opened on December 13, 1958, Killington was just one more hill.

What makes this so hard to believe? Consider, if you will, a few present-day facts:

• Skiing Killington means skiing six separate mountains, all connected by trails and lifts.

• Killington has 77 miles of alpine ski trails. Mount Snow, the second largest Vermont ski area, has 32.

• Killington owns Mount Snow.

• Killington has 18 lifts: six double chairs, four triples, five quads (including two new detachable quads), two surface lifts and a 3.5-mile gondola, the longest ski lift in North America.

• The gondola services the 10-mile Juggernaut, the longest alpine ski trail in North America.

• Killington also has the longest chairlift in North America.

• Killington also has the longest ski season in the East, and, with the exception of a few peaks in Oregon and one isolated mountain on Uranus, the longest season in the galaxy.

• Staying at Killington? There's room for 4,800 at the base of the mountain; more than 15,000 in the region.

• Killington's parent corporation recently bought Goldmine Ski Area, 90 miles east of Los Angeles. It immediately changed the name to Bear Mountain. Given Killington's propensity for expansion, it's only a matter of time before its public relations department (The Public Relations Department That Never Sleeps) announces that the world's longest chairlift stretches from the Green Mountain State to Sushi City. Lift tickets will cost $700.

• When an inch of new snow falls on Killington Peak at midnight, by nine the next morning every ski writer in the country has heard about it, from The P.R.D.T.N.S.

• When an inch of new snow doesn't fall on Killington Peak, the resort's massive snowmaking operation, the most extensive in the world, goes into high gear. Killington makes snow on 40 miles of its trails. Stowe — once the biggest ski resort in the East — makes snow on 13. (Contrary to popular belief, snowmaking wasn't invented at Killington. But don't bother explaining that to your friends; they simply won't believe you.)

• Snow grooming wasn't invented at Killington either, but it might as well have been. In the course of a night, Killington grooms the equivalent of a seven-lane highway from Rutland to Boston. In the course of a season, it grooms more than 100,000 miles of trails, roughly four times around the equator.

And that's not all, folks. In addition to all that skiing on a longer trail than anywhere else, with a longer lift than anywhere else, for a longer season than anywhere else, with more snowmaking than anywhere else, Killington has also pioneered creative ski instruction.

Its most significant innovation was the Graduated Length Method, begun in the mid-1960s. For the first time, a ski school institutionalized the idea that learning would be a lot easier if novices didn't begin skiing on 210-centimeter skis. It's amazing no one thought of it before. Sure, skiers usually slap boards as tall as their upraised arm on their feet, but there's no law that says they have to learn that way. Killington started new skiers on waist-high skis and advanced them to longer lengths as they progressed.

This evolved into the Accelerated Ski Method in which individual components of skiing are taught on a specially prepared area. Killington, which is known for its fearsome steeps, also has some of the gentlest learning terrain anywhere.

In 1982 the Accelerated Ski Method was expanded to intermediate skiers with the introduction of Mountain Training Stations. Skiers stop off beside the trail to learn bump skiing or slalom turns from waiting instructors. Most skiers love it, largely because:

• *It's a lot looser than most traditional ski classes.*
• *It lets individuals choose what they want to learn.*
• *It works.*

To put Killington in a nutshell, you need a pretty big nutshell. Even an attempt to capture its many moods requires a minimum of three visits — early season, mid-season and May. Here's a sample of each.

Skiing Early

Snowmaking is a mixed blessing. Machine-made snow at its best doesn't reach the quality of natural snow at its best. Skiing in front of a snow cannon is as deafening as walking behind a jet engine. And the silent beauty of ski slopes at night is a thing of the past. Thanks to snowmaking machinery, ski slopes howl the whole night long.

But the advantages of snowmaking outweigh all that. The chief advantage is that ski seasons open earlier and close later than dreamed possible when natural snow was all there was to rely on. And Killington has pushed the ski season to its furthest extremes.

Killington defies any competitor to match its season in length. Most years it's open for business from mid-October through the beginning of June. Halloween, Thanksgiving, Easter, Memorial Day — all are ski holidays at Killington. Only Labor Day and the Fourth of July have — thus far — eluded the resort's snowmakers.

In October, day tickets are sold at a discount since skiing is limited to relatively few trails. But it's not the discount that brings the crowds; it's the certain knowledge that this is the only game in town. Impatient enthusiasts flock to Killington from all over the region, clogging the open trails with more moving bodies than they can comfortably accommodate. On their way into the parking lot, early-season drivers are handed a printed warning that demand will outweigh facilities. But the area still sells tickets to all comers.

Some of the early birds don't appear overly grateful for the discount price. As one skier grumbled, "They also accept second mortgages."

But grateful or not, they zoom down crowded slopes, hurtle over any bump they can find, and crash into each other like carnival bumper cars. Try not to blame them — Killington in October has an effect on skiing fanatics similar to that of rutting season on elk.

Skiing Mid-Season

You're standing at the top of the fabled Outer Limits, and you are struck by the thought that you don't know what to call it. Too wide for a trail, too long for a slope, and too steep and bumpy to possibly get down, you're stuck for a descriptive word and a safe route to the bottom. All around you, bump busters are yahooing their way over the lip, dropping deep into gullies, then jetting into the blue sky off the leading edges of elephantine moguls. Finally, you give up trying to name this species of terrain, collect what's left of your nerve, and take the first step on that long way down.

Thanks to a midwinter thaw, the sun is warm, the snow is soft, the bumps are forgiving, and you suddenly discover you're having fun. To your surprise, you hear a small "yahoo" escape your lips, followed by a longer and louder one. You're skiing. You're flying. You love Killington.

Now it's the next day, and you're on another Killington peak, looking down another slope, Mouse Trap. The thaw has disappeared, taking with it any trace of sunshine. Yesterday's soft, inviting snow has frozen solid in the night. You're gazing apprehensively at a sheet of blue ice, and you know that your edges wouldn't hold even if your nerve did. Cramped from tension, you inhale and start a clenched muscle traverse across the rock-hard surface. Two teeth-jarring minutes later you discover that you've forgotten how to ski. You've also forgotten to exhale. You hate Killington.

It's late in the third and final afternoon of your Killington trip. The sun is setting on a day in which the thermometer has climbed back into plus figures. Thanks to snow in the night, the ice has been replaced with powder, light at the top of Superstar and heavy at the bottom. You're tired but happy from a frown-proof day spent skiing all six peaks. You've ridden the gondola, the Northeast Passage triple chair (the only one you've ever seen that runs downhill as well as up), the South Ridge chair (the only one you've ever seen that hangs a sharp left halfway up the hill), even the Snowshed chair, which services beginners' slopes. And now you've ended your six-mountain quest on the Superstar detachable quad. It's been exhausting, but it's been worth it to have skied all six of ... all six — oh, no! You do a quick finger count and confirm what you feared — not only have you missed one, you've neglected to ski the big one, 4,241-foot Killington Peak itself. How humiliatin'!

You're driving home, going over the past three days and laughing at the thought of skiing Killington and missing Killington Peak. You think as you drive just how different this trip was from other ski vacations. Killington dances to a faster beat, sings in a louder voice than other areas. It's bigger, younger, more impersonal, more exciting, more frustrating, more ... it's more, more, more of everything. You re-experience the feeling you had at the top of Outer Limits, smile and shake your head. You love Killington.

Skiing May

Superstar isn't an easy trail at the best of times. Late May isn't the best of times.

At least for most skiers it's not; for hotdogs, bump busters, and mogul mavens, it's totally awesome, the ultimate!

It's a late May Sunday, and you and 246 other skiers, most of them young, male and athletic, pay a $10 lift fee and board the chairlift at the bottom of Skye Peak.

It's summer at the base. Trees are in full bloom, and golfers are teeing off at the nearby course. On the chair just in front of you, tennis players in white shorts are boarding the lift with boxes of sandwiches for a picnic on the peak.

As you ride the lift you pass from summer to spring before the halfway point. Above 2,000 feet, trees are just coming into bud, and the temperature, although still in the mid-50s, is noticeably lower than at the base. Still, you can't see even a small patch of snow or one other skier; only the occasional hiker trudging up the grassy trail beneath the lift.

But two-thirds of the way up the mountain the chair passes over a snow-covered trail. It's Superstar, rated "Expert" in winter and posted "For Advanced Skiers Only" in spring. The sign is right. You're looking down on a steeply inclined plane that spring skiers have turned into a mass of dips, ruts, and bumps. Ski Killington — ski the moon.

And now you see the skiers. The bumps are big enough to loft them into the hazy sky, where they're performing splits, holding poses, and twirling their way through 360-degree turns. Their expressions are of dazed blissfulness. You hurry off the lift, ready to go.

But getting to the snow isn't easy. First you take off your skis, then scramble down through 50 yards of mud and scree to where the snow begins. You're in colorful company — above their muddy boots, your fellow skiers are dressed in Bermuda shorts, tank-tops, bathing suits and wildly hued T-shirts. Their median age is 18. Their median body build is mesomorph. Their median expression is an uncontainable grin.

By the end of your first short run, you know why. Despite the warm weather, the snow is in great shape, and it's at least two feet deep. This apparent violation of natural law was accomplished by "stockpiling" snow on the trail all winter long. Since early February Killington's snowmaking guns have been turned on, producing giant "whales" — great hump-backed mounds of snow. By late March the whales were more than 20

Killington

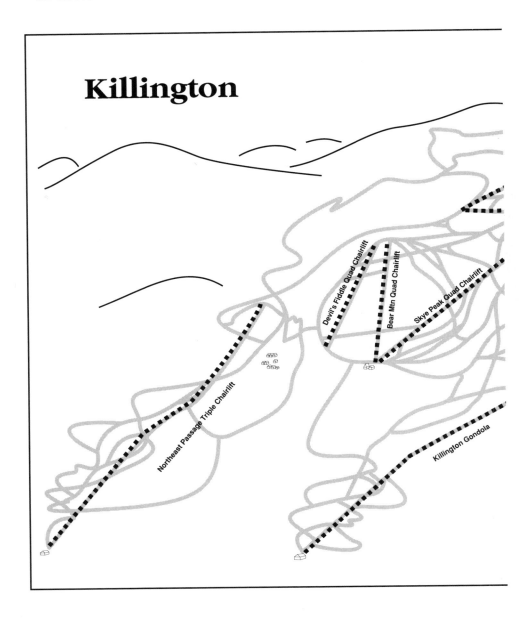

feet deep. Now, you're skiing on their remains.

Awesome, you think, awesome. It's the only word that even begins to cover the pleasures of this day. The whole thing would be perfect . . . Well, the whole thing would be perfect except that every time you stop

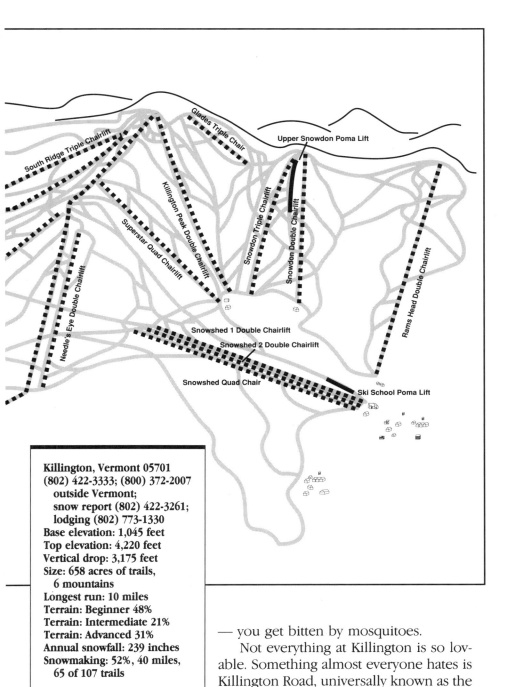

Killington, Vermont 05701
(802) 422-3333; (800) 372-2007
    outside Vermont;
    snow report (802) 422-3261;
    lodging (802) 773-1330
Base elevation: 1,045 feet
Top elevation: 4,220 feet
Vertical drop: 3,175 feet
Size: 658 acres of trails,
    6 mountains
Longest run: 10 miles
Terrain: Beginner 48%
Terrain: Intermediate 21%
Terrain: Advanced 31%
Annual snowfall: 239 inches
Snowmaking: 52%, 40 miles,
    65 of 107 trails

— you get bitten by mosquitoes.

Not everything at Killington is so lovable. Something almost everyone hates is Killington Road, universally known as the

Access Road. Ecologists and engineers alike have only harsh words for its built-up, commercial, glitzy look.

But there is another viewpoint. Killington is a big, commercial and glitzy area. Its patrons need places to sleep, eat, dance and be glitzy. Those 15,000 beds have to go someplace — they can't all be hidden behind pine trees. And it's fair to say that most of the lodges, restaurants and emporiums along the road are designed to fit the look of a major ski resort. There are no high-rise hotels or flashing signs, just a lot of woodsy, glassy buildings.

Here are some examples of what's around for glitzing:

Mother Shapiro's is where Killingtonians eat breakfast. It's got a New York Jewish schtick, meal portions sized with hungry skiers in mind, and it opens at 6:30 a.m. When you want something hot and tasty, head down to Charity's for their famous onion soup. For lunch, try Powderhounds or Pogonips in the Snowshed Base Lodge. Dinners are fine at Claude's, the Grist Mill, and the Summit.

If you want to go a little further afield, Hemingways, east along Route 4 toward Woodstock, is famous for classic cuisine and formal service. It also happens to be one of New England's outstanding restaurants. Eight miles south on Route 100, the Hawk River Tavern serves creative combinations, including goat-cheese pizza and snails baked in red-skin potatoes.

After-dinner entertainment? Most ski resorts, from California to the coast of Maine, are a disappointment in the entertainment line. The brochures promise swinging singles bars where you can boogie all night and blast your inner ears into oblivion, but when you get there, you find a little old man playing "O, My Papa" on an accordion. Somewhere at Killington there may be a little old man pushing a squeeze box, but there are plenty of other alternatives.

The best known is the Wobbly Barn. Big, brassy, loud and, on midwinter weekends, more crowded than a box of raisins, the Wobbly has been packing 'em in with live music since Killington was a one-hill resort. On Tuesdays they give away skis as a door prize. Didn't win a pair? Head down the road to the Pickle Barrel. It's nearly as loud and crowded and gives away skis on Thursdays. The Night Spot is another dance hall, but with disco instead of a live band. There's no shortage of piano bars and subdued trios in and around Killington and plenty of pubs where you can have a quiet drink and conversation.

. . . .

KILLINGTON is a glitzy, expensive, tremendously varied and enormous ski area whose ambition is to become a super-enormous ski area. If the past is any guide to the future, it soon will be.

TIP: On busy weekends, the least crowded place to ski is the Northeast Passage on Sunrise Mountain. It has its own chairlift, parking lot and base lodge, all just south of the intersection of Routes 4 and 100.

KIDS: As you might expect, Killington has a full range of child-care and teaching options. There's day care for children from 6 weeks to 8 years, an introduction-to-skiing program for 3- to 8-year-olds, and the Superstars Program for skiing kids from 6 to 12 years old. Kids even have their own adult-free learning area.

WHERE: The Killington Access Road begins off Route 4 about 12 miles east of Rutland, in south-central Vermont.

Chapter 8
Mad River Glen
A Skier's Mountain, Pure and Simple

A folklorist collecting the countless skiers' stories about Mad River Glen would discover two recurrent themes: "This mountain is different from any other" and, from Mad River regulars, "This mountain is better than any other!"

Here are a few Mad River stories — all true — that illustrate what's different about Mad River, and may help explain the pride of its loyal patrons. The first tale is about a long-distance phone call.

A middle-aged skier returning to Vermont after years away telephoned Mad River Glen to book a ski week. As middle-aged skiers often do, he began to reminisce. "Yessir," he said, "it was 1963. That was the last time I skied Mad River. I know you guys pride yourselves on not changing, but I'll bet even at Mad River there have been a lot of changes since '63."

There was a long pause. Finally, the staffer said, "Hmmm. Since '63? No, I can't think of any."

The story's true, but the staffer's facts weren't quite right. Like every area, Mad River has changed and improved over time. New trails have been cut, new groomers bought. But unlike most areas, Mad River doesn't like to talk about change. It prefers to cling to tradition.

In an era of four-passenger chairlifts, Mad River still operates a single-chair lift. In an era of broad boulevards running straight as the Jersey Turnpike from the peak to the base lodge, Mad River still has hand-cut trails snaking through the woods. In an era of grooming snow to the texture of a velour bedspread, Mad River still leaves many of its trails untouched. And at the beginning of the 1988–89 season, when most American ski areas were vying for the distinction of having the newest snowmaking system, the most expensive winch cat or the fastest ski lift, Mad River Glen, on the eve of its 40th anniversary, issued this bulletin: "Two thousand bales of hay were spread over the trails to induce and create top soil on the steepest part of the trails."

While others were spending millions, Mad River was spreading hay.

This raises a question: How can a determinedly low-tech, no package, no hotel, one restaurant, one ski lodge, hayseed ski area that still runs a single chair to the summit survive when it's right next door to Sugarbush and down the road from Stowe? The answer is that there are enough purist, old-fashioned and/or hotshot skiers out there to support it — who wouldn't have it any other way.

Most Mad River Glen skiers would bitterly resent wide trails, perfect grooming and "après-bloody-ski nightlife." They want to know that in 2001 they won't see any changes in their beloved Mad River Glen or in General Stark Mountain, on which it resides.

Mad River Glen is a skier's mountain, pure and simple. Its trails are mostly steep and twisting. Its ambiance is rough and ready. Its lifts are basic. Its snowmaking is non-existent above the 2,200-foot flurry line. (On the other hand, its snow grooming is advanced.)

Mad River has always been that way, and a lot of folks hope it always will be. It was founded in 1949 by Roland Palmedo, who wanted to get away from what he saw — in the 1940s — as the growing commercialism of Stowe. Its five original trails (which, four decades later, remain essentially unchanged), were designed and cut by mountain manager Ken Quackenbush.

The present owner, Betsy Pratt, and her husband, Truxton, bought one of the first ski houses in the Mad River Valley in 1954. In 1972 they bought the mountain.

Three years later, "Trux" died. Betsy, living in Connecticut and raising four children alone, found herself the owner of a ski mountain in northern Vermont. "I begged our manager, Ken Quackenbush, to run the area until I could stop being a full-time mother. After he retired as president, I took over. He still consults for me."

According to Betsy Pratt, Quackenbush is the genius behind Mad River. "He designed most of the trails," she says, "and also established the attitude that the trails must flow into the contour of the mountain."

General Stark Mountain, with its 33 trails, four lifts and 2,000 vertical feet of skiing, is Mrs. Pratt's main interest. She says, "I want to preserve the mountain. It's the mountain that brings us together, not the sport. Fifty or 100 years from now there will be new ways to enjoy the mountain, ways we haven't yet dreamed of. I want the mountain to be there for those generations."

To understand Mad River Glen, you not only have to understand its outspoken owner, you have to understand its outspoken skiers. They're different from other skiers in a number of ways.

First, there's that intense loyalty. The true Mad River skier doesn't think there's any other skiing in the state — and adamantly refuses to believe in Aspen. To what other mountain in the galaxy would skiers come in the summer and, working without pay, spend sweaty days cutting undergrowth? To what other mountain in the known universe would skiers come in the fall, pay to take the chairlift to the top, then hike down, throwing loose stones into the woods?

Second, Mad River skiers are fanatics about natural snow, as opposed to what they still sneeringly refer to as "artificial snow." They swear that the nasty artificial stuff turns icy as soon as it gets warm, isn't bio-degradable and probably causes cancer in chickens.

The third thing about Mad River skiers — and this is important to

understand — is that they're insane. The place is aptly named. The mad skiers of Mad River ski past trees, through bushes, brambles, hobblebush. They ski over ice, rocks, ledges, cliffs, waterfalls. Any piece of mountain — whether it sports a trail marker or not — is fair game at Mad River. There's plenty of glade skiing, but it's hard to tell the glades from the woods since both are full of skiers.

As you ride up the single chairlift (vintage 1948 and still running smoothly), you're likely to see some young warrior whipping down through the woods. He skis happily along until a large branch, lying just under the surface of the snow, clears his ski tips, then clips his ankles and puts him flat on his face. For some reason, the young warrior

gets up smiling, and as soon as he's cleared his mouth of snow exclaims, "Awesome!"

"Awesome" is the best word to describe Fall Line, one of the most beautiful trails at Mad River or anywhere else. But beware of the trail's last 200 yards, affectionately known as the Creamery. It's just low enough on the mountain for ice to form overnight. Then a fresh inch of powder camouflages it beautifully. A favorite trick of long-time Mad Riverites is to watch new skiers confidently blast into it — and get creamed.

Mad River's management, now as always, keeps the trails sown with grass to prevent erosion. Since Roland Palmedo, Ken Quackenbush and both Pratts have all seen themselves more as environmentalists than resort people ("this is not a destination resort!" snaps Betsy Pratt), the grass sowing and hay spreading become understandable. So does the reluctance to cut trees. Mad River is one of the few areas left in the East that leaves islands of trees in the middle of its trails.

The area is equally recalcitrant about widening or straightening trails, about bulldozing ledge or altering the contours of the mountain. Says Betsy Pratt: "I want to preserve it for future generations, not blast it into submission or let it erode."

Mad River is among the least commercial ski areas anywhere. Another story illustrates the point: it took place on a Sunday when snow cover was light and traffic was heavy. Rather than subject patrons to long lines and rapid build-up of ice, Betsy Pratt simply "hid" 70 spaces in the parking lot, forcing that many cars to drive past Mad River to Sugarbush North.

The area's motto — "Ski It If You Can" — is somewhat misleading. Although it reflects Mad River's commitment to an all-condition, all-terrain skiing experience, it gives the impression that you have to be an expert to handle the trail system. In fact there is very nice terrain from high-beginner through hotshot. People with very little experience can ski comfortably from the mid-station of the single chair down Fox and Vixen or take Porcupine over to the Birdland chair, which serves all-beginner terrain.

But it should be noted that the only way to get to that beginners' terrain is from halfway up the mountain. And any area that has its beginners' slope high enough so that you have to ski down to reach it just may be making a statement.

At the bottom of the slopes, the Base Box, built in 1948, still serves as the core of the base lodge. The building, ahead of its time by about 40 years, was designed to be warmed by passive solar heat. In it is General Stark's Pub, home of outstanding hamburgers and onion soup thick and cheesy enough to be a lunch in itself.

The most obvious place to stay when skiing Mad River is the Mad River Barn, within skiing distance of the mountain. It's an old-fashioned, knotty pine ski lodge with kerosene lamps on old oak tables and the expectation of pot roast at the 6:45 seating. It's a reasonable expectation, but very, very wrong. Instead, fare includes such delights as cream-of-artichoke-heart soup, sautéed duck breast with blueberry sauce, scallops with vodka and crème fraiche, and mocha rum cheesecake, all at reasonable prices.

Mad River Glen is now in its fifth decade. Although it's not alone among the old-timers that have reached that grand age, how many others could honestly claim that a number of the original employees are still

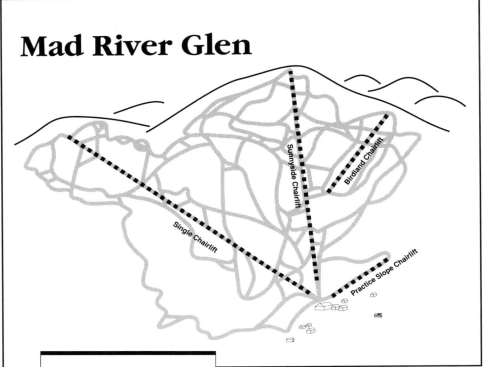

Mad River Glen

MAD RIVER GLEN
Fayston, Vermont 05673
(802) 496-3551;
snow report (802) 496-2001
Base elevation: 1,600 feet
Top elevation: 3,600 feet
Vertical drop: 2,000 feet
Size: 85 acres of trails
Longest run: 3.5 miles
Terrain: Beginner 25%
Terrain: Intermediate 40%
Terrain: Advanced 35%
Annual snowfall: 200 inches
Snowmaking capacity: 15% of
skiable terrain

working there — or that many of the original patrons are still skiing there?

• • • • • • • •

MAD RIVER is a big and beautiful mountain, with narrow and surprising trails, a striking absence of snowmaking and an ambiance all its own. Inexpensive lift tickets and a ski school specializing in private instruction. Skiing as it once was. A legend.

TIP: A good way to get to know Mad River is to ride the single chair and work your way across Stark Mountain from right to left. You'll start on relatively easy trails and get into progressively more difficult terrain as you warm up. Another tip: Mad River is part of Ski Vermont's Classics, which means Classics passholders can ski there as well as at Jay Peak, Bolton, Sugarbush, Stowe and Smugglers' Notch.

KIDS: Mad River has a full-service nursery for tots from 3 weeks and up. Its ski school offers the SKIwee program for children from 4 to 12. Accompanied children 5 and under ski free.

WHERE: Mad River Glen is on Route 17 in central Vermont about five miles west of Waitsfield and 20 miles south of Montpelier.

Chapter 9
Magic Mountain
Lots of Steep, Lots of Variety, Lots of Fun

When Simon Oren bought Londonderry's Magic Mountain in the mid-1980s, most ski areas were falling all over each other in the rush to identify themselves as family resorts. Oren surveyed the field and said, "Anytime I hear that, I think of a dull place to be. I want Magic to be where single skiers and young couples come to ski hard and party hard and have fun."

Oren no longer owns Magic — he sold it to Bostonians Bob Palandjian and Joe O'Donnell in 1988 — but there's enough of his brash style left for it to remain something of a maverick among mountains. Of course families enjoy Magic, just as they do every ski area in Vermont, but its day care program is limited.

For hard skiers, though, the mountain is nothing short of, well, magic. Although it has a beginner's chairlift and Magic Carpet, a lilting low-intermediate trail from the summit, Magic Mountain specializes in providing thrills and chills for advanced and expert skiers.

For advanced skiers, two extra-nice trails are First Trick and Talisman. First Trick rates a black diamond, but when it's groomed it's really a high-intermediate run with enough pitch to keep the adrenaline pumping. Talisman is steep, straight and scary. To get to it, make your way down an attractive catwalk called Voo Doo. But before you reach Talisman, glance over the side of the trail. That nearly vertical, rock-strewn cliff is Master Magician, unarguably labeled double black diamond — for experts only. Are you ready for it? If you get a nosebleed just looking, that's nature's way of telling you you're not.

By the way, you may not see a trail sign for Master Magician; lack of signs is one of Magic's shortcomings. (It has another sign problem that we'll look at shortly.)

As you stand on Voo Doo wondering if you'll ever be brave enough or foolish enough to tackle Master Magician, you'll see the trails of two other ski areas to the west. The bigger one is Stratton; the other is Bromley, Magic's sister mountain. (Magic and Bromley are under the same ownership.)

52

Continue along Voo Doo (which shortly becomes Wizard) until you come to Talisman, an expert trail that starts narrow, then widens into a sharply inclined slope, broad enough to let you turn your way out of the fall line. Halfway down it changes its name to Mistral.

(If you wonder whether all this name changing is some sort of Magic disappearing act, it's actually just the opposite. It's an *appearing* act. Ski areas do it to create the illusion of more trails than the eye can see. Magic Mountain is by no means the only area to perform this trick; like the rabbit from the hat, it's a staple of the trade.)

To the left of the two summit chairs is Magic Carpet, a glorious 2.5-mile swing through the woods that is suitable for low-intermediates and up. Well-designed and maintained, it's a hoot for moderately competent skiers and a thrill for novices. From Magic Carpet, or from the exceptionally comfortable Mid-Mountain Triple Chair, you can swing onto High Anxiety or Vertigo which, though relatively short, have enough pitch to justify their names.

On the subject of names, the area's trails began with magic themes — Magic Carpet, Harry Houdini, then switched to movies — High Anxiety, Vertigo, then Hawaiian — Maui and Diamond Head. There's also a Swiss connection — Swiss Connection — and a Jewish one — Goniff. Does this bespeak an identity crisis or just cultural pluralism? The conflicting Swiss and Vermont architectural styles duking it out at the bottom of the hill point toward the former.

Magic Mountain has no less than 10 double-diamond trails snaking their way down the hill. Most require pretty good natural snow cover before most moderately sane individuals would chance them. But one is almost always skiable — Maui, which runs into the mogul-strewn Diamond Head. Both trails have earned their diamonds, and those who ski them earn their pride. The mountain's other expert trails are equally worthy of their double-diamond designation. The glades — particularly Goniff — may be worth a triple. Skiing Goniff is like leaping into a briar patch turned on its side. Don't even think about trying it without a lot of snow on the ground.

Magic Mountain

Timber T-Bar

Timber Chairlift

MAGIC MOUNTAIN
Londonderry, Vermont 05148
(802) 824-5566;
  snow report (802) 824-5566
Base elevation: 1,300 feet
Top elevation: 3,000 feet
Vertical drop: 1,700 feet
Size: 177 acres of trails
Longest run: 2.5 miles
Terrain: Beginner 25%
Terrain: Intermediate 50%
Terrain: Advanced 25%
Annual snowfall: 150 inches
Snowmaking capacity: 78% of
  skiable terrain

Even when there's not much snow, the area's snowmakers and groomers take excellent care of their terrain. Their strategy is to make one heck of a lot of snow on a modest number of trails rather

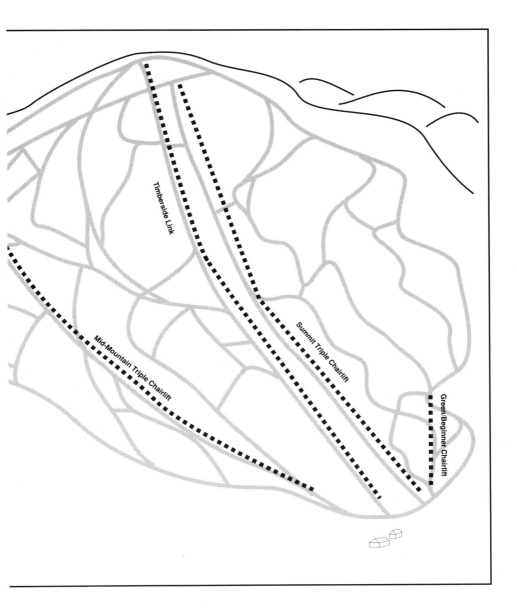

than thinly spread a small amount over the whole mountain. Given the state of the art of snowmaking, it's the right approach. Instead of a plethora of marginal skiing, Magic skiers find a moderate amount of excellent skiing even when no snow at all has fallen from the skies.

Magic is a particularly innovative ski area. An example is its rotating grooming system. What's smooth as silk one day may look like a steep freeway full of Volkswagen Beetles the next. So before you try a trail, take a good look down it first. If the moguls are as big as Volkswagens, you'd better be pretty good at skiing Volkswagens.

Another caution — when getting off the Timber Chair for the first time, try to relax. The exit ramp is short, but it's nearly vertical, and the sudden drop-off may take you by surprise. The trick is to just let it happen; there's adequate run-out to keep you out of the trees.

In 1986 Magic Mountain purchased Timberline, a defunct private ski area. Through some clever trail building and land leasing arrangements, they hooked it onto the Magic trail system via Magic Pass, a three-quarter-mile-long trail along the ridge. Timberline, renamed Timberside, has its own double chair, base lodge and T-bar. It offers old-fashioned narrow trail skiing, a remarkable absence of crowds and an ambiance all its own. Unfortunately, its rustic atmosphere is somewhat sullied by big outdoor beer and cigarette ads around the base lodge. That's the other sign problem.

Magic has many charms, though. It's a substantial mountain with a 3,000-foot summit and a 1,700-foot vertical drop. It's crosshatched with skillfully cut trails that offer a challenge to even the best skiers. What's more, the trails are creatively groomed and artfully snow-covered. The fact that Magic and Bromley tickets are interchangeable makes both mountains more of a bargain.

Another big plus is the mountain's location in the Golden Triangle of Vermont skiing, the region with Magic, Bromley and Stratton at its corners and a plethora of eating and shopping options in between.

· ·

MAGIC MOUNTAIN is a medium-big, medium-to-high-priced, creatively run mountain designed with serious skiers in mind. Lots of steep, lots of variety, lots of fun, and for lovers of old-time skiing, Timberside.

TIP: If you suspect it's going to be a crowded day, park at Timberside and start skiing from there. You'll beat the crowds in the parking lot, at the ticket counter and on the lift.

And an outside tip: Route 11, which runs from Manchester past Bromley and Magic, is among the best patrolled of Vermont's well-patrolled highways. When that smiling trooper pulls you over for speeding, don't tell him Jules sent you.

KIDS: Magic's day care program accommodates a relatively small number of 3- to 5-year-olds. Better call well ahead for a reservation.

WHERE: Magic is off Route 11 in Londonderry in southern Vermont.

Chapter 10

Mount Snow

The Giant of the South

The first thing that strikes you about Mount Snow is how big it is. Here you are at the bottom of Vermont, just 25 miles north of Greenfield, Massachusetts, and you find yourself looking up at a serious ski mountain with four separate faces (including the little-known and very sunny south face), 18 lifts (including a detachable quad), 84 trails (including some real expert terrain), extensive snowmaking (enough for the second-longest season in Vermont), and a 1,700-foot vertical drop.

You were planning just to take it easy on this first day — do a little snowpiking, see some country sights, try a new restaurant — but you look again at the mountain and experience a familiar itch. The sun is shining, there's a light breeze blowing from the west, and, staring down at you is all that snow. Suddenly, driving and eating seem silly. Frivolous. A poor use of precious time.

You're in the throes of ski fever. On with the boots, into your bindings, choose a lift. But which lift? In this mood, there's only one choice — Yankee Clipper, the high-speed detachable quad that will whip you to the top faster than anything else on the mountain. When you arrive, slipping into your pole straps as you come out of the chair, you're faced with a much tougher choice — where to take your first run.

You should warm up on a long, easy trail like Deer Run, 2.5 miles of mellowness.

You're not in the mood for mellow.

Then why not head for the sunny blue squares on the Sunbrook area?

You don't have time for sun or squares. Your eyes swing to the North Face trail markers. Plummet. Free Fall. Jaws of Death.

Jaws of Death? No, you're not that crazy. Yet. Instead, you turn to the main mountain, point your skis back under the chair, and start down Exhibition — one and a half miles of wide, varying terrain coming straight down the liftline. It's labeled More Difficult, but it's got enough challenge for the hottest ticket on the hill. And considering your febrile state, that just might be you.

Down you go, opening with a series of quick slalom turns, setting your edges hard, keeping your speed in check. Then, as you pass the top of the Ego Alley chair, you start using all the width of this wide trail. You switch into great, swooping giant slalom turns, carving long, elegant S's in the packed powder. By the time you whoosh past the skiers unloading from the Beaver triple chair, you're catching air on every bump. Your eyes are watering, your heart is racing, your thighs are burning, your knees are begging for mercy, and your soul — your soul is knocking at heaven's gate. Ski fever strikes again!

The beauty of Mount Snow is that even this far south, surrounded by palm trees and flocks of flamingos, there is enough solid skiing to cure the worst case of ski fever. Even better, there's so much mountain here, you can take the week-long, month-long or life-long cure and never be bored. Better still, Mount Snow has so much terrain at all levels of difficulty that an entire family of fevered skiers with widely differing abilities can have a blast.

Having a blast is exactly what Mount Snow was designed for back in 1954. It was the brainchild and love child of one Walter Schoenknecht of New Haven, Connecticut. When he died in 1987, Schoenknecht was hailed as one of the great visionaries of skiing. But in 1954, when he transformed farmer Reuben Snow's upper pastures on Mount Pisgah into Mount Snow Resort, he was reviled.

B.S. (Before Schoenknecht), skiing was the preserve of the fit and wealthy. Outsiders were barely tolerated. Beginners were scorned. Skiing was a small and exclusive club you practically had to be born into to be accepted. Enter Walter Schoenknecht, a big man with bigger ideas and an ego the size of the Matterhorn. He decreed that skiing should be fun — fun for experts, fun for beginners, fun for snow bunnies whose only contact with snow was on their way into the après-ski pub. What's more — what's worse — he decreed that the pleasures of skiing should not be reserved for those to the manor born but should be extended to the hoi polloi ... even unto New York City secretaries.

There can be no doubt Schoenknecht was a visionary. In 1949, while managing a Connecticut ski area, he hauled in 11 truckloads of ice which he proceeded to crush and spread on the slopes. The next year he installed the country's first snowmaking system on those same slopes. And in 1954, in the obscure village of West Dover, Vermont, he opened Mount Snow.

The skiing world had never seen its like. At the base of the mountain, Schoenknecht built a 13-acre artificial lake, and beside the lake he built a hotel. To get from hotel to mountain, he installed a gondola, which he called an "air car," and which slowly carried skiers past a fountain in the middle of the lake, a fountain that transformed itself into a massive ice sculpture in winter.

Was there more? There was more: Japanese dream pools. A heated outdoor swimming pool. A sundeck on the roof of the ski shop overlooking the pool. An indoor ice rink. A restaurant filled with tropical vegetation. Live bullfrogs croaking in the tropical vegetation. He planned (but never built) a motel with a trampoline in the lobby and a hotel with a real mountain stream running through the dining room.

Yet all these toys and ploys were tiny compared to his ego. "In the ski business, I admire myself above all others," he said. "I've got an uncanny knack for sensing what skiers want and the imagination and resolute drive to produce it."

He was right. Novices, never-evers, never-will-be's, snow bunnies and hordes of New York secretaries flocked to Mount Snow, quickly turning the resort into what he predicted it would be all along — the world's busiest ski center. His detractors, amazed and dismayed by the phenomenon they were witnessing, called Mount Snow the Coney Island of the Snow Belt. They called Schoenknecht the Abominable Snowman.

Like so many visionaries, W.S. was better suited to creating a phenomenon than running one. After a series of snowless years in the mid-1970s, Mount Snow filed for bankruptcy. In 1977 it was purchased by the Sherburne Corporation (now S-K-I, Limited), the owners of Killington, who rapidly set about Killingtonizing the area — getting rid of the fat and trimming the operation down to lean, mean efficiency.

The Japanese dream pools were drained. The swimming pool was filled; the ice rink melted. The fountain and air cars were dismantled. Snowmaking increased from 7 percent of the mountain in 1977 to 80 percent today. The grooming fleet grew from two Tucker Snocats to nine Pisten Bullies and a winch cat. Lift capacity nearly tripled. In four years the resort was breaking even. Today S-K-I, Limited is the most profitable ski resort company in Vermont.

By 1986 Mount Snow was strong enough to expand, buying its nearest

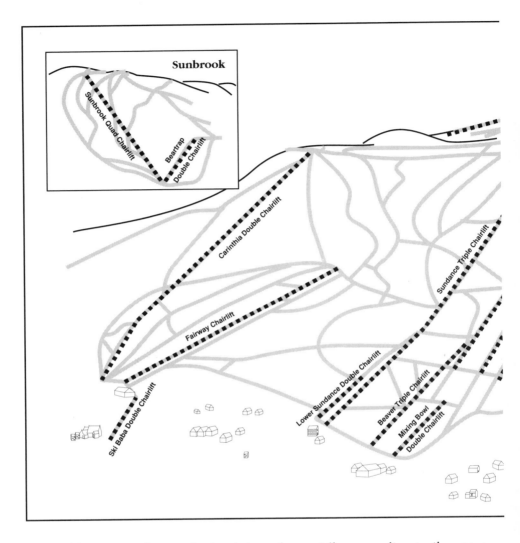

neighbor, Carinthia, and tying it into the rapidly expanding trail system. Today you can ski from gentle Carinthia over to the Main Mountain, then across to the scary runs on the North Face, then to sunny Sunbrook and finally back to Carinthia again. If you take only a couple of runs on each face, you've put in a full day's skiing. And you can go back tomorrow and do it all again, skiing entirely different trails.

Should you want a break from all this skiing, there is no shortage of things to do in the Mount Snow region, sights to see and, especially, meals to eat. Since the mountain is so close to Haystack, check that

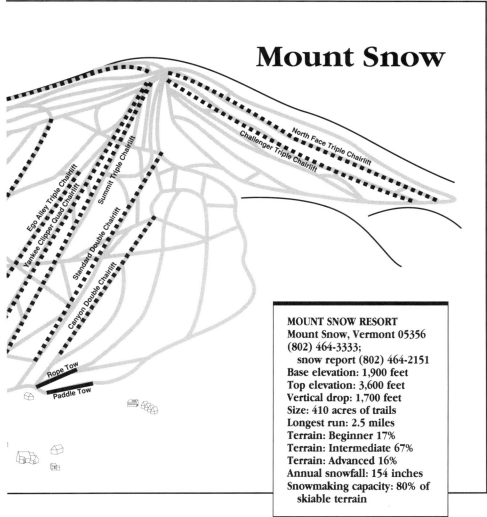

Mount Snow

North Face Triple Chairlift

Challenger Triple Chairlift

Ego Alley Triple Chairlift

Yankee Clipper Quad Chairlift

Summit Triple Chairlift

Standard Double Chairlift

Canyon Double Chairlift

Rope Tow

Paddle Tow

MOUNT SNOW RESORT
Mount Snow, Vermont 05356
(802) 464-3333;
**   snow report (802) 464-2151**
Base elevation: 1,900 feet
Top elevation: 3,600 feet
Vertical drop: 1,700 feet
Size: 410 acres of trails
Longest run: 2.5 miles
Terrain: Beginner 17%
Terrain: Intermediate 67%
Terrain: Advanced 16%
Annual snowfall: 154 inches
Snowmaking capacity: 80% of
**   skiable terrain**

chapter, too, for recommendations.

There are places nearby for cross-country skiing, horseback riding, sleigh rides and snowmobile touring. There are fitness centers at Snow Lake Lodge and Seasons Condominiums, a game farm at the Hermitage, a historic country store museum and a bowling alley. There are enough antique, art, craft and specialty shops and galleries to keep the most dedicated shopper hopping like a mogul maven in March. As for food, the Inn at Sawmill Farm is justifiably famous, Two Tannery Road is a favorite with local gourmets, the Roadhouse and Deerfield's are reasonably priced and good, and Snow Lake Lodge offers a $6 breakfast with a $6 million view. For dancing the night away, the Snow Barn and Deacon's Den are the spots that are hot.

Finally, here are a few observations about the giant of the south, Mount Snow.

• The Mixing Bowl chair at the bottom of the hill is a piece of ski history, a holdover from the mid-1950s that is still running strong.

• The Ski Baba chairlift, servicing the beginners' area by the Carinthia base lodge, has a vertical rise of exactly 50 feet.

• Mount Snow is the exception to the rule that trail marking gets more

generous the further south you go. Here, black diamond means Most Difficult, no doubt about it.

• If you want to evaluate the black diamond trails on North Face without actually skiing them, take River Run from the Standard Chair. It runs along the bottom of the steep stuff, allowing a cool, safe judgment before you tackle trails with names like Jaws of Death and Ripcord.

• Ripcord is the scariest of the lot, a 1,300-foot-long mogul field tilted like the back of an unloading dump truck. Should you find yourself at the top and have a sudden revelation that you shouldn't be, there is a way out that doesn't involve taking off your skis or staging a nervous breakdown. Just to the right is the aptly named Second Thoughts, which offers a considerably kinder, gentler descent.

• If you're renting skis or taking a lesson, you can buy your lift ticket at the shop or ski school without having to line up at the ticket windows.

• While it is widely accepted that Mount Snow and Killington are among the most commercial ski operations anywhere, it's interesting to note that neither allows billboards on its trail markers or condos on its trails.

. . . .

MOUNT SNOW is a very big, very varied, very southern, fairly expensive resort surrounded by fine restaurants, interesting lodges, craftsy shops and caressed by tropical breezes.

TIP: From Mount Snow's director of communications, Laurie Croot, here's a way to save time and trouble at this vastly popular resort: "On weekends, don't buy your tickets at the main lodge — in fact, turn off before you reach it. Carinthia Lodge is still undiscovered. Parking is easy, lines are short, and if all you need are lift tickets or rentals, you can take care of all your business there."

KIDS: There's an all-day SKIwee program for children 6 to 12 and a Peewee SKIwee program for 4- and 5-year-olds. Day care accommodates children from 6 weeks to 12 years. During Mount Snow's five Teddy Bear Ski Weeks, kids who bring their teddy bears ski free and get to participate in a lot of activities. Movie and pizza nights are every Wednesday.

WHERE: Mount Snow is on Route 100 about nine miles north of Wilmington in southern Vermont.

Chapter 11
Okemo Mountain
Well-Groomed, Upscale Cruising

Okemo Mountain Ski Resort is, at one and the same time, genuine success story and a genuine paradox.

First, the success. From its beginnings in 1956 until the summer of 1982, Okemo was a small, struggling ski area with a few Poma lifts, a rough warming hut and an almost entirely local clientele. It was the kind of place where everyone knew everyone else in the lift line by first name ... but that was partly because there was no real reason to come there from anywhere else. For out-of-state skiers, Okemo was the mountain you passed on the way to Killington.

That was until the summer of 1982, when Tim and Diane Mueller bought Okemo Mountain and began its transformation. Today, it is unrecognizable to those who skied there in its early days. From a local hill, Okemo has grown into New England's third biggest ski resort in skier days — 400,000 in 1989–90. Only Killington and Mount Snow attract more skiers.

Where Pomas once ran, eight chairlifts and two surface lifts whisk 16,400 skiers per hour onto the slopes. Okemo Mountain's once puny snowmaking system is now plugged directly into the Black River, giving it a capacity greater than any Eastern area except Killington and Mount Snow. The resort pays as close attention to the care and grooming of snow as any ski area in New England. And for all this, Okemo's once cheap lift ticket is now among the most expensive in the East.

As Okemo Mountain has grown, so has the region. Ludlow's old mill is now an upscale shopping center and condo complex. Aged farmhouses and declining village mansions have become country inns and ski club dorms. Restaurants have sprung up, and with them antique stores and ski shops. In Singleton's store, five miles from the base of the mountain, locals and Connecticutites wish each other Merry Christmas while buying home-smoked ham. A few minutes away, Joe Cerniglia has transformed his apple orchard into New England's biggest — and best — winery.

That's the success story. Now the paradox.

Despite its new facilities, high price, upscale image, and its great care of trail and snow, Okemo Mountain has made two decisions that compromise skiing pleasure and the mountain experience.

The first is easily correctable. For reasons best known to corporate accountants, the resort has let its trail signs double as billboards. In this otherwise billboard-free state, it is disconcerting to pay for a lift ticket, stand at the top of a snow-covered mountain and then be subjected to outdoor ads for chocolate bars and chewing gum. One of the pleasures of skiing is the feeling of leaving the rest of the world behind — actually, below. Chewing-gum ads bring it right back up.

The second problem is less correctable. In its desire to raise capital and to build a housing base for patrons, Okemo Mountain has turned hillside, slopeside and trailside into housing developments.

The condos surrounding the base lodge are fine. They're clustered around the hub of commerce and activity that is the heart of the resort. Those at the top of the South Ridge chair are more marginal. Instead of gazing into the woods, lift riders find themselves looking into apartment windows. But when they get off the lift, they leave the buildings behind.

If these two developments are within tolerable limits, what can be said about the neighborhood that abuts — and at times actually intrudes into — some of Okemo Mountain's ski trails? Coming down Upper Sachem and Lower Sachem is like skiing through Scarsdale.

Even when viewed from Ludlow, the houses and condos — there are over 200 in the Trailside complex alone — detract from the image of the mountain. They further detract from the pleasure of skiing, at least for those who enjoy the illusion of getting away from it all. Construction continues, and were it not for Vermont's Act 250, which forbids building above the 2,500-foot level, the trailside neighborhood would undoubtedly stretch to the summit.

Fortunately, most of Okemo's trails are still forested, not neighborhooded, and they give skiers a special bonus. The bonus is that when you ski Okemo, you're likely to find yourself skiing better than you ever have in your life.

Why? A small part of it is trail designation. At Okemo, as at many southern Vermont areas, what is called black diamond (Most Difficult) terrain would be labeled blue square (More Difficult) further north. So if you're skiing the black diamond Upper World Cup (a long and lovely trail with lots of steepish pitches followed by natural resting places), you may decide you're an expert after all.

But the main reasons skiers step up a notch at Okemo have little to do with trail markers and everything to do with trails. They are unusually well laid out — wide enough to accommodate lots of skiers practicing easy turns, yet curvacious enough to retain at least an impression of the New England tradition of paths winding through the woods. What's more, they are a tribute to the snow-groomer's art.

Okemo Mountain's groomers, many of whom have worked there long enough to know the mountain like their own driveways, are among the Enlightened Ones who understand that difficult concept — variety. Some trails get the shag carpet treatment. Others are left as ungroomed mogul

fields. And a fair number are kept in-between.

It's the in-betweens that hold the key to skiing pleasure. Once ski areas have proved they can groom the roughest mountain terrain into the consistency of velvet, they need to follow Okemo's lead and ease off, leaving some of their snow semi-groomed, preserving enough contour to keep skiing interesting.

Another advantage Okemo has capitalized on is its broad-sided mountain. You take one lift, the South Ridge chair, up a sloping valley. From there, you ski down to one of the six mountain lifts. This set-up has two benefits.

First, you needn't return to the base lodge until the end of the day. Thanks to the Sugar House, a large cafeteria near the base of the mountain chairlifts, you can even take a lunch break on the slopes. If you're really in a hurry, you needn't even bother with that. At the foot of the Solitude chair is Solitude Station, a kind of outdoor Meals on Wheels where you can grab a kebob or a bowl of chili and eat on the lift. If your edges wear out before you do, right by the Sugar House is a weekend/holiday ski tuning tent at which you can get a quick sharpening or hot waxing without standing in line at the repair shop.

The second benefit is this: because the mountain lifts are spread across the side of the hill, so are the skiers. Even on busy weekends, the Solitude area is likely to be uncrowded, as is the shorter Green Ridge triple chair.

On the subject of chairs, Okemo's are fast, well maintained and remarkably comfortable. The lift attendants are skilled, smiling and helpful. The lifts are as well cared for as the snow. Once you reach the top, spend

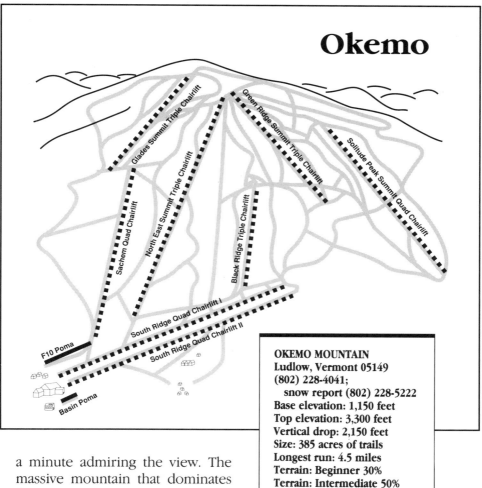

Okemo

Glades Summit Triple Chairlift

Green Ridge Summit Triple Chairlift

Solitude Peak Summit Quad Chairlift

Sachem Quad Chairlift

North East Summit Triple Chairlift

Black Ridge Triple Chairlift

South Ridge Quad Chairlift I

South Ridge Quad Chairlift II

F10 Poma

Basin Poma

OKEMO MOUNTAIN
Ludlow, Vermont 05149
(802) 228-4041;
   snow report (802) 228-5222
Base elevation: 1,150 feet
Top elevation: 3,300 feet
Vertical drop: 2,150 feet
Size: 385 acres of trails
Longest run: 4.5 miles
Terrain: Beginner 30%
Terrain: Intermediate 50%
Terrain: Advanced 20%
Annual snowfall: 200 inches
Snowmaking capacity: 90% of
   skiable terrain

a minute admiring the view. The massive mountain that dominates the eastern horizon is Mount Ascutney. Looking north from Mountain Road, a 4.5-mile beginner's trail, you can see the south side of Killington.

On the mountain you can eat at the attractive Priority's or at the cheap and funky Dadd's pub. Or drive down the access road to Ludlow, a town with a number of good restaurants and delis. DJ's is known for modest prices and immodestly large scallops. Nikki's and the Potbelly Pub are local favorites. Michael's specializes in seafood and does a delicious Seafood Louisiana. Chuckle's, too, has a southern influence — its Cajun shrimp are great. The Hatchery and the (ahem) Café at de Light serve the best breakfasts in town. The Depot Street Delicatessen sells the best sandwiches for miles — and they deliver!

If you're staying on the mountain, you'll be staying in a condo. The 76 one-bedroom units that rim the base area are collectively called the Okemo Mountain Lodge. They're clean and comfortable but not spectacular. Further up the hill, most of those trailside homes are also for rent.

If you cast a wide enough net, you'll find plenty of old-fashioned inns within 10 or 15 miles of the mountain. Right on Main Street in Ludlow are the Black River Inn and the Governor's Inn. The more rural Echo Lake Inn and the Combes Family Inn are a few miles out of town. The elegant Castle Inn and the Golden Stage Inn are in Proctorsville. The much praised Inn at Long Last is in Chester.

Full information about lodging is available through the Okemo Mountain Lodging Service at (802) 228-5571.

· ·

OKEMO has some black diamond glade skiing (generously labeled double black diamond), but for the most part this is an upscale, expensive mountain designed for beginners, intermediates and cruisers rather than thrashers, thrill seekers and adrenaline junkies. Some trails are gentler, some are steeper, but nearly all are wide, well groomed undulating and fun. Nature, with a little help from the Muellers, designed Okemo with high- and low-intermediate skiers in mind.

TIP: When the slopes get crowded, try the Green Ridge triple chair and the Solitude area.

Another tip, the Secret of True Parallel Skiing, first experienced at Okemo Mountain: I've always turned by planting my pole and lunging around it. This lunge has taken many forms over my years of skiing. An upper body twitch, an uphill hop, a soft-shoe shuffle — all served to get me into the turn, and all kept me locked in a bloody stem.

What I discovered on Okemo was that if I just waited a second, my skis would ski around the turn by themselves. All I had to do was wait! Initiate the turn, wait, then let the skis turn by themselves. Magic.

What do you do during the wait between pole-plant and turn? Well, I unweight, point my knees in the direction of the turn, then whistle the first few bars of Beethoven's Fifth. You may prefer a different tune. But however long it seems to take (in reality it takes a second or less), wait until the skis are ready to take you with them.

Now why did it take me so long to learn that?

KIDS: Okemo has long been known for offering carefully supervised child care. Here are the options: Day care is for 1- to 8-year-olds; 3- and 4-year-olds get an introduction to skiing with their care. SKIwee is for children from 4 to 8, with a full or half day on snow and indoors. The children's ski school teaches those age 7 and up, grouped by ability. And the Young Mountain Explorers is for those with intermediate and better ability who are between 8 and 12.

WHERE: The access road for Okemo starts just west of Ludlow on Route 100/103 in south-central Vermont.

Chapter 12
Pico

Still Friendly After All These Years

Talk about ups and downs. While every ski resort has its good years and bad, Pico Ski Resort really goes to extremes. At one time it was among the premier resorts, not just in Vermont, but in the United States. It had the first alpine chairlift in the state, the fastest ski racers in the East, the first volunteer ski patrol in the country, the longest trail in the world.

But Pico didn't stay at the top. While other mountains surged ahead, Pico remained small, old-fashioned, and — the bottom line — unprofitable.

Three factors kept this resort near Rutland from resurfacing at the top of Vermont skiing. The first was tragedy.

The area was started in 1937 by Brad and Janet Mead, a young couple who combined wealth, individualism, vision and ski madness in roughly equal measures. It was they who made Pico the mecca of Vermont skiing in the 1930s, the only rival to Stowe in the 1940s, the scourge of opposing ski teams through both decades, and the most European, i.e., advanced, American area during this country's formative years of skiing.

In the Winter 1946 issue of *Vermont Life,* Janet wrote: "After absorbing a part of the loveliness of the Vermont hills throughout the changing seasons, our skiing enthusiasm grew to magnificent proportions ... To have a sport which would create the desire to get into the snowfields ... to enjoy the cold tang of sunshine-filled wintry days ... to have the physical benefits of the exercise in skiing plus the wonderful camaraderie found among the followers of this great sport, all this totalled in our minds great progression."

But the great progression came to a sudden halt when Brad died at age 37 in a boating acccident. He was buried near the summit of his beloved mountain. Janet carried on alone for years, eventually selling the resort to Karl and June Acker. Karl, whom the Meads had brought from Europe to run their ski school, now became the man in charge of everything on the mountain. In 1958, at age 42, he died of a heart attack. Like Janet Mead before her, his widow was forced to struggle on alone.

She ran the mountain single-handedly until she sold it in 1964.

After tragedy, the biggest impediment to Pico's future was sewage.

In Vermont, sewage is a serious matter. Before anyone builds or expands a venture of any real size, the state wants to know what plans they've made for disposing — safely and inoffensively — of their sewage. For years Pico, which is in the watershed that supplies the city of Rutland's municipal reservoir, couldn't figure out what to do with its, and consequently the resort could not expand. Finally, in 1982 the board of directors bit the bullet and organized construction of a privately owned sewage pipe that ran the nine miles from the mountain, down along Route 4, all the way into Rutland. It was only then that expansion began, and the mountain started to awaken from its years of slumber.

There was another factor that kept Pico out of the spotlight. Its next-door neighbor is the Jolly White Giant, Killington. As New Zealand is to Australia, Canada to the United States, Smugglers' Notch to Stowe — Pico is to Killington, and living next to a giant, no matter how jolly, isn't easy. In Pico's world this meant that however early they opened, however much new equipment they installed, however much money they spent on promotion, Killington would be earlier, bigger and better-heeled.

Nevertheless, like New Zealand, Canada and Smugglers', you can still carve out your own identity, and indeed you'd better if you're going to survive.

Pico capitalized on what it had. It dubbed itself The Friendly Mountain, and made sure that families knew their kids would be well cared for. The fact that all lifts lead back into the same bowl helped: If you don't know where your children are, just wait at the bottom until they show up. At other mountains, they could be on up to six different peaks or God-knows-how-many lifts leading to God-knows-where.

And once Pico solved its identity problem and got its sewage act together, it did three things to ensure parents would bring their progeny to The Friendly Mountain rather than continue up Route 4 to Killington. They built condominiums — 132 of them — at the base of the hill. They built a big, modern sports complex next door to the condos. And they built state-of-the-art lifts to carry all those families up to the peak of the mountain. Two of New England's nine detachable quads are at Pico.

In addition to the building program, the resort went out of its way to offer innovations that would make skiing more affordable. It invented the Sunday morning ticket that allows you to ski until noon and still stand a reasonable chance of making it home before dark. Pico gives beginners up to four hours of complimentary skiing. Informal morning and afternoon classes show new skiers how to get in and out of skis, get on and off of lifts, how to turn, stop, and, of course, go. Ski school director Joe Wood says, "That first time out on skis can be stressful. Our program is designed to take some of the pressure off." Wood has assembled a team of highly qualified instructors to ensure the pressure stays on the downhill ski.

All this was designed to improve Pico and to make it more competitive with Killington. But there is something beyond competition, and that is consolidation. Since 1990 Pico has been planning to merge with Killington to create one of the largest ski complexes in the United States (and may have already done so by the time you read this.)

What's it like to ski The Friendly Mountain? Pure pleasure. There's even something pleasing about Pico's nearly symmetrical cone shape. Viewed from afar, it's instantly recognizable. Gliding down its sides simply feels good. From the 3,957-foot summit of Big Pico you gaze over to Killington's western trails, down to Magic and Stratton, across to Lake Champlain and the Adirondacks, up to Stowe. Once you've finished soaking in the view, you choose your way down.

The most obvious choices are Forty-Niner and Pike, two broad, beautifully maintained boulevards running from top (in the case of Forty-Niner, almost-top) to bottom. Pike follows the liftline of the Summit Express detachable quad and has a very respectable pitch for its first 200 yards. Forty-Niner is approached via the prettily wooded Easy Street and despite its black diamond designation is kind to skiers the whole way down.

Both trails are designed to convince you you're a better skier than you thought you were. It works. One thing that helps is that grooming is taken very seriously at Pico. If there's snow on the ground, they'll have it in good order for skiing. Another aid to advancement is the abundance of excellent skiers to emulate. Pico regulars know how to move, partially because of the proximity of the mountain to Rutland area high schools, partially because its racing program is still running strong. You won't find any "Slow Skiing Area" signs at Pico; fast, controlled skiing is the

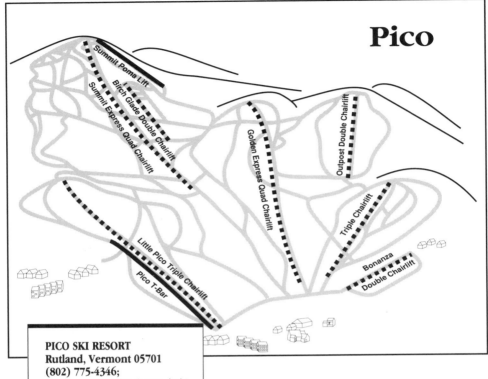

Pico

PICO SKI RESORT
Rutland, Vermont 05701
(802) 775-4346;
   snow report (802) 775-4345
Base elevation: 2,000 feet
Top elevation: 3,957 feet
Vertical drop: 1,967 feet
Size: 183 acres of trails
Longest run: 2.5 miles
Terrain: Beginner 22%
Terrain: Intermediate 50%
Terrain: Advanced 28%
Annual snowfall: 200 inches
Snowmaking capacity: 82% of
   skiable terrain

norm all over the mountain.

Whichever trail you choose, you can predict its configuration with assurance. The top quarter of the mountain is steep, though not strike-terror-into-your-heart steep. The middle half is moderately pitched, perfect for carving giant slalom turns down the wide trails. The bottom quarter is a long run-out, a chance to get your breath back before heading up for another run.

Should you tire of Big Pico, skate over to Little Pico, the original mountain the Meads developed. The chair carries you up the same line their historic T-bar once followed. As you glide over the ultra-steep liftline, consider what it was like for T-bar riders struggling to keep their skis on snow as they were pulled up the hill. (Actually, lighter ones didn't keep their skis on snow. The lift was famous for giving air on the way up.) On the way down, Little Pico has a pair of gnarly mogul slopes that will keep your mind off any business other than the business of firing off short-radius turns.

If you're staying at Pico, the obvious place to spend your evenings is at the Pico Inn, which is actually the condominiums at the base of the hill. They're bright and attractive, and most come equipped with a fireplace. Next door is the sports complex, complete with large lap pool and high-tech exercise equipment. Eating out, you can get a pizza, a waffle, a cocktail or a full meal without leaving the mountain.

Down the road, Rutland has a number of special places to eat, including Ernie's Bar and Grill, a/k/a Royal's Hearthside, one of the region's landmark restaurants. Downtown (and upstairs) is the Back Home Café, another favorite among Rutlanders. Between Pico and Rutland, Route 4 is a highway of restaurants, including the highly regarded Vermont Inn, Sugar and Spice, and Countryman's Pleasure (just off Route 4 on Town Line Road).

. . . .

PICO is friendly, fun, historically important, moderately difficult and reasonably expensive. It takes the "Friendly Mountain" slogan seriously. The staff is helpful and well informed. The place is small enough to be called intimate, yet varied enough to keep most skiers happy for a long time.

TIP: The first half hour at Pico, from 8:30 to 9:00, is free every day. The idea is to let skiers test conditions before investing in a ticket.

KIDS: Pico offers certified day care for ages 6 months to 3 years. For ages 4 to 12, there's supervised ski instruction and/or play. Instruction is structured according to ability. The Pico Children's Center also hosts a kids party on Saturday nights during holidays.

WHERE: Pico is on Route 4 about 10 miles east of Rutland in south-central Vermont.

Chapter 13

Smugglers' Notch

An Alpine Village and a Fine Ski School

In 1956, when Smugglers' Notch first began life as a ski area, it was a strictly local affair owned by a group of Cambridge businessmen who first opened it only on weekends. Called Smugglers' Notch Skiways, its trail system on Sterling Mountain was serviced by a couple of rope tows and two Poma lifts.

Ah, Poma lifts. The Poma lift is a metal platter about the size of a dinner plate, affixed to the bottom of a thick metal pole. The top of the pole is attached by a coiled spring to a constantly running overhead cable. Today, most of the few remaining Pomas serve gentle beginners' slopes, but back in the 1950s, they often climbed the whole mountain. The Mountain Poma at Smugglers' was a classic. You got on, grabbed the pole with one hand and nodded to the operator. At your signal he pulled a lever releasing your platter. When he did, you held your breath, planted your ski poles and pushed. The top of the spring grabbed the cable, and off you went on a solitary ride up the mountain.

But should you forget to watch the operator or forget to plant your poles, your trip began very differently. When the spring grabbed the cable, you were suddenly lifted off the snow with a powerful lurch that carried you through the air for the first 10 feet of the journey.

But it was worth it. Smugglers' upper lift, which ran over a mile to the summit ridge, offered silence, solitude, and beauty. Approaching the top, you were carried across a snow-covered bridge and into a silent forest of snow-laden firs. Getting there was half the fun.

The peaceful quiet of the lift typified the area. Smugglers' then was a lot like Burke now. But all that changed in 1964 when Tom Watson Jr., chairman of the board at International Business Machines, took over Smugglers' Notch with the intention of turning it into an Eastern Vail — a self-contained village centered around skiing and tennis. He tore down the Pomas and put up chairlifts, including what was then America's longest lift, on Madonna Mountain. To commemorate the event, he changed the name of the area to Madonna Mountain Corporation.

Then, in 1973, Watson sold out to Stanley Snider, who had designed the village with him. Snider expanded the resort and changed the name again, this time to The Village at Smugglers' Notch.

Whatever name it went under, the area suffered from being on the wrong side of the mountain from its bigger and more sophisticated neighbor, Stowe. During the years when Stowe was the undisputed Ski Capital of the East, Smugglers' never entirely escaped the shadow of Mt. Mansfield.

Another shadow over Smugglers' Notch was the reputation of paying more attention to off-snow development than to the care and feeding of its ski trails. The resort was said to be long on condos and amenities and short on snowmaking and trail grooming.

Both shadows have receded in recent years. Stowe is no longer the epicenter of Eastern skiing, and Smugglers' Notch has come a long way in caring for its mountains. Although its snowmaking is still behind most of its competitors, and its lift system is stretched beyond capacity on busy weekends, in recent years its snow grooming has been right up there with the best.

Where Smugglers' Notch really shines is in its ski school, one of the most imaginative anywhere. That imagination is easiest to see in the children's program.

Operating on the concept that guiding the body is as important as instructing the brain, the school has pioneered the concept of the terrain garden. That means they've fashioned parts of the mountain into teaching tools. For children as young as 3, the terrain garden is the main method of teaching. It's a zone filled with cut-out animal figures inviting young skiers onto gentle slopes molded in such a way as to force them into proper ski positions. Bumps, ridges, chutes — all do the teaching in place of words.

For adults, there are now three mountains at Smugglers' Notch, all interconnected and all accessible from the village. Beginners' classes wedge their way down the wide slopes of Morse Mountain. Intermediate classes are on Sterling, the original mountain from Poma lift days. Hotshots ski Madonna. High winds at Madonna's peak often close the longest chair, but even without it, there's a broad range of trails, from upper intermediate to extremely hairy expert.

At the heart of post-Poma Smugglers' is The Village at Smugglers' Notch. It sports a swimming pool, ice rink, tennis courts, saunas and steam baths, restaurants and nightclubs, sleigh rides and movies, and enough condominiums to make it look like Yuppie Heaven.

Embodied in the village are two keys to Smugglers' success. One is that the community is small, safe, convenient and self-contained. Residents walk to the store, the nightclub, the pool — and the chairlift. The second is that Smugglers', like a growing number of Vermont ski areas, has turned itself into a four-season resort. It offers tennis in summer, foliage in fall, skiing in winter, and conference facilities in spring.

There are two main groups of patrons. Families are the mainstay of the area and come in ever-increasing numbers. January is college month, when students from all over the East arrive to ski all day and party all

night. Management wisely keeps the students in one set of condos and families in another. The result is peaceful coexistence, on the slopes and off.

Smugglers' Notch specializes in putting together packages. Student packages include lift passes, lessons, swimming, skating and parties. Family packages include free child-minding, kids' ski lessons, sleigh rides, a coloring book and the Cookie Monster Challenge Race. During Family Fest weeks, diners at the Village Restaurant drop off their kids for a supervised dinner, arts and crafts, and entertainment while the parents enjoy a meal to themselves.

Adding to the resort's family appeal is the recently completed Alice's Wonderland, a child care center certified to accommodate up to 95 children. Named after director Alice Boyer, the center is set up for children from 6 weeks to 6 years. Sometimes kids get their first ride from Alice's to the slopes on a horse-drawn sleigh. Non-skiers enjoy the horses, too; Smugglers' has its own stables and a petting zoo.

The result of all these inducements to families and students is an area with kids of all ages floating about the village and the slopes. It's a nice feeling, at least for those whose idea of a ski vacation isn't getting away from kids of all ages. It's only negative side is rock music blaring out at the bases of the chairlifts and the occasional too-loud, too-late party.

For frequent skiers, Smugglers' Notch sells the Bash Badge, which entitles the bearer to major lift-ticket savings any day of the year, holidays included, as well as discounts on lessons, rentals, indoor tennis and ski shop purchases. It also entitles them to free use of the ski area's pool, sauna and hot tub.

Once you've bought your ticket, what's it like to ski the Notch? With three big mountains, the choices are many.

Most skiers begin the day on Morse Mountain because its Village Lift is within walking distance of the condos. But day skiers not needing rentals or beginners' lessons do better by driving past the village entrance and parking in one of the upper parking lots. From there it's a reasonably short hike to the Sterling and Madonna lifts.

All three mountains offer skiing for intermediate skiers and experts, but only Morse has real novice trails. Most hotshots scorn Morse, but they're missing Upper Lift Line, a broad, bump-infested boulevard that has brought more than one skier to his or her knees. Garden Path and Sam's Run are considerably more forgiving ways down Morse Mountain, and for those still afraid of "going to the top," the chair has a mid-station exit that leads onto the wide and easy Lower Lift Line as well as the terrain garden.

On Sterling, the long-standing favorite for intermediates is Rumrunner, named in honor of the real smugglers who gave Smugglers' Notch — the pass between Jeffersonville and Stowe — its moniker. Getting to Rumrunner means surviving the Wind Tunnel, a breezy and sometimes icy chute that leads into it. Be not afraid! Once you're through that, the worst is behind you. The rest of Rumrunner is easier, less icy and considerably more fun.

Smugglers' big mountain is Madonna, 3,610 feet above sea level. High intermediates love Chilcoot, which spills off the top and swings wide over the broad rim of the mountain before rejoining the trail system at Father Bob's Run. On a clear day, when hoarfrost covers the trees and the trails on Mt. Mansfield stand out in bold relief, the view is nothing short of inspirational.

On Madonna, experts ski the steep and narrow FIS, the double black diamond (super expert) Lift Line or the well-named and even steeper Freefall. Freefall has a 54 percent gradient; skiing it is like jumping off a tall building.

After sampling three mountains, you've probably worked up a fair hunger. Here's where you can relieve it:

In the village, the Crown and Anchor is a deluxe restaurant with carefully prepared meals served in the atmosphere of an English pub. Next door, the Village Restaurant is a large and attractive room that specializes in family dining and whose food ranges from pretty good to very good.

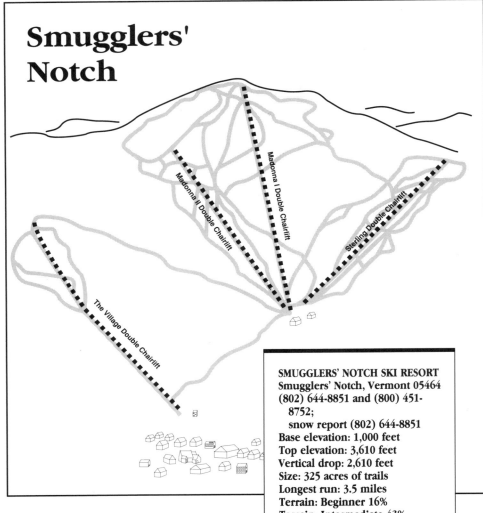

Smugglers' Notch

Madonna II Double Chairlift

Madonna I Double Chairlift

Sterling Double Chairlift

The Village Double Chairlift

SMUGGLERS' NOTCH SKI RESORT
Smugglers' Notch, Vermont 05464
(802) 644-8851 and (800) 451-8752;
snow report (802) 644-8851
Base elevation: 1,000 feet
Top elevation: 3,610 feet
Vertical drop: 2,610 feet
Size: 325 acres of trails
Longest run: 3.5 miles
Terrain: Beginner 16%
Terrain: Intermediate 43%
Terrain: Advanced 41%
Annual snowfall: 260 inches
Snowmaking capacity: 45% of skiable terrain

Half a mile down Route 108 is Brewski, a lively, sometimes rowdy, pizza joint equipped with the requisite video games and pool table. The most exciting off-slope restaurant near Smugglers' is Le Cheval D'Or at the Windridge Inn in Jeffersonville; its food has been praised up and down the state. And at the corner of Routes 15 and 108 is a real find. The Cupboard makes outstanding sandwiches, bakes its own pastries, sells New Zealand beer and serves authentic Greek spinach pie — all modestly priced, and all "to go." Next door is Jana's, where you can get the same quality and price and a table as well.

Most skiers at Smugglers' Notch stay in the village. Those who don't can get a list of lodges and motels from the Chamber of Commerce, P.O. Box 364, Jeffersonville, VT 05464, (802) 644-2239.

One hostelry that is both special and inexpensive is the Red Fox Alpine Lodge. Two miles from the mountain, it's a dorm-style lodge with home cooking and down-home friendliness. Over in Cambridge, the Cambridge Castle Bed and Breakfast is an aptly named Queen Anne mansion, circa 1894, that would look like a haunted house if it weren't for its cheerful yellow paint. In Jeffersonville, the Smugglers' Notch Inn has been receiving guests since the mists of antiquity.

• • • • • • • • • • • • • • • • • •

SMUGGLERS' NOTCH is a self-contained village at the base of three impressive mountains, the biggest of which has a 2,610-foot vertical drop. It's got a lot of expert terrain and an innovative ski school with special programs for children. Smugglers' is a fairly expensive area except for Bash Badge holders and package dealers.

TIP: From Sherm White, assistant ski school director: Try an early morning run down Chilcoot on Madonna. On a clear day you have the White Mountains on your right, the Adirondacks and Lake Champlain to your left, and a constantly changing vista in front. Chilcoot is full of personality. It has an intermediate rating, with all manner of dips and twists and turns. You can exercise your full range of skills without getting in over your head. The morning light and the freshly groomed slope add to the fun.

KIDS: Smugglers' specializes in children's programs. The Discovery Ski Camp for 3- to 6-year-olds includes ski sessions, mountain games, sleigh riding, storytelling, cookie racing and creative snow play. It also includes cocoa breaks and a hot lunch.

Seven- to 12-year-olds go to Adventure Ski Camp. Supervised all-day activities include ski instruction, fun races, mountain adventure games and ski treks. Campers also get a hot lunch.

Discovery and Adventure kids can attend an educational program in the late afternoon. They learn about the weather as well as the mountains and the critters who inhabit them.

Thirteen- to 17-year-olds can enroll in the Explorer Ski Program, which begins with instruction and goes onto racing, plus broomball, snow soccer and tube races.

The Smugglers' Guarantee promises that kids will have fun during Family Fest weeks. If they don't have fun, their parents receive a refund of that portion of their vacation package devoted to the kids camps. The conflict this must raise in parents who want to see their darlings enjoy themselves but also would love a refund check, must be almost too great to bear.

WHERE: Smugglers' Notch is on Route 108 just south of Jeffersonville in the north-central part of the state.

Chapter 14

Stowe

A Mighty Mountain with a Great Tradition

The day is cloudy, and as you turn off Route 100 and onto the Mountain Road it grows cloudier still. By the time you reach the Mt. Mansfield parking lot, you can't see Mt. Mansfield. Maybe today's the day to stay inside by the fire.

But the snow report said the hill was covered with packed powder and you've driven all this way, so what the heck. Take the skis off the roof rack, buy your ticket, buckle your boots and head for the Forerunner quad. Settling into the chair, you glance at the cloud bank squatting 100 feet above you and wonder if you've made a mistake.

Two minutes later, as the bank swallows you and cuts visibility to five yards, you're sure you did. The snow may be packed powder, but you'll need a miner's light to make it down through the fog. You ride for the next six minutes in moist silence, wondering what it is about skiing that brings out the fool in you.

A hundred yards from the top, you get your answer. The chair suddenly emerges from the clouds, and you find yourself blinking in the brilliant sunshine. The snow is so white it makes you squint through your goggles. The rocky cliffs that tower over the lift sparkle with reflected light. Above them, the sky is all that blue can be.

You take a deep, appreciative breath and become aware of an anticipatory tingling in your fingertips. You've never seen a day so clear, a landscape so sharply outlined, a mountain so majestic. Just as you prepare to leave the chair, you experience a fleeting pang of sorrow for loved ones who don't ski and a moment of sadness for those who do ski but aren't with you today at Stowe.

You're not the first to experience these feelings. For most of this century, Stowe was the place — *the* place — to ski east of Sun Valley, Idaho. The area made its first move toward becoming "The Ski Capital of the East" on February 22, 1921, the date of the first Stowe Winter Carnival.

Some would date Stowe's skiing origins considerably earlier. Just after the turn of the century local craftsmen fashioned a few skis from hardwood boards. In 1914 the first recorded ski descent of Mt. Mansfield was accomplished. And around 1915 a Swedish immigrant family taught the rudiments of skiing to interested local kids. But it wasn't until Washington's Birthday, 1921, that the idea of skiing as a tourist attraction caught on.

Trying to ease the gloom of the postwar economic depression, a few townspeople organized a winter carnival on that date. The event was a great success. In brilliant sunshine, a thousand spectators gathered to

watch "20 big competitive events" including snowshoe and toboggan races, half-mile and 220-yard ski dashes, and ski jumping on the newly constructed jump. So popular was the evening minstrel show that after the gallery and aisles filled to capacity, they sold sitting space on the radiators.

But after a series of snowless winters and a summer storm that demolished the ski jump, the carnival petered out until 1932. That year a new 300-foot ski jump was built, along with toboggan and bobsled runs. By 1933, the carnival included slalom and cross-country races and, as a special attraction, an exhibition by a Norwich University student of ski jumping on one ski.

In the 1930s, the Civilian Conservation Corps was helping America out of the Great Depression by planting forests and building dams, roads, and parks. Craig Burt, who owned a hotel on the summit of Mt. Mansfield, and Perry Merrill, an avid skier and director of Vermont's Forests Department, managed to persuade the CCC that ski trails were roads. Thus it came to pass that in 1933, the Civilian Conservation Corps cut the Bruce Trail, the first trail on Mansfield.

The next summer a second trail was cut, one that was to give the mountain its reputation for tough skiing. The trail was Nosedive. It's still in service, though in somewhat gentler form after being widened and tamed in 1966. The first ski patrol in the country was formed at Stowe in 1936, and more trails were carved out of the mountain through the rest of the decade.

But the event that put the seal on Stowe's skiing leadership took place in 1940. The nation's longest chairlift was started that summer and completed in the fall. The 6,300-foot single chair was designed to carry 200 skiers per hour, but at its unofficial opening, it carried no skiers per hour. With a load of press people and VIPs on board, the lift ground to a halt and refused to be coaxed into further movement. All passengers had to be evacuated.

Despite its inauspicious opening, that pioneering lift and the many that followed ensured Stowe's place in skiing history.

Today, Stowe is no longer the giant among giants; Killington has taken over that role, with Mount Snow and once-miniscule Okemo close behind. But Stowe still has its share of superlatives: the tallest mountain in the state (4,393 feet), the most trails in the North (378 skiable acres plus 150 kilometers of cross-country trails), a great variety of lifts (with a combined capacity of 10,000 people per hour), an entire mountain (Spruce Peak) just for beginners and intermediates, and some of the best skiers anywhere.

They're drawn by Mansfield's long, steep trail system. The biggest pull is exerted by the fabled Front Four: Starr, National, Liftline and Goat. The best word to describe the lot of them is vicious.

Their pitches begin at 35 degrees and work up. Starr is a minefield of bumps, the kind of place you look down and pray it will be closed for the day. Goat is narrow as a snake. National is a pool table tilted on its end. Liftline is perfect for those who get their kicks from public humiliation.

And skiers love every one of them.

Nosedive is nearly as tough as the Front Four, but that's not enough for some. Rugged types turn left, de-ski, and climb above the official start of the trail so as not to miss the narrow, nasty turns at the top. Crazy types turn right and ski down to a snowfence erected to keep patrons off a cliff-like drop. Setting their ski tips on a couple of broken slats, they leap the fence and hurtle down through the air, rejoining Nosedive at its first wide point, where Stowe's famous Sugar Slalom is held each March.

Not everything on Mansfield is killer-steep. Hayride is merely challenging, and Tyro more pleasure than pain. Whichever trail you choose, you may be sure it is not overrated. If the sign says black diamond, it's for advanced skiers. If it says double black diamond, it's for the well-insured.

The easiest trail on the mountain is Toll Road, a nearly four-mile meander that eventually makes its way down to the Toll House Double chairlift and the Touring Center. But most beginners don't ski Mansfield at all; instead, they drive or take the shuttle bus to Spruce Peak. Easy

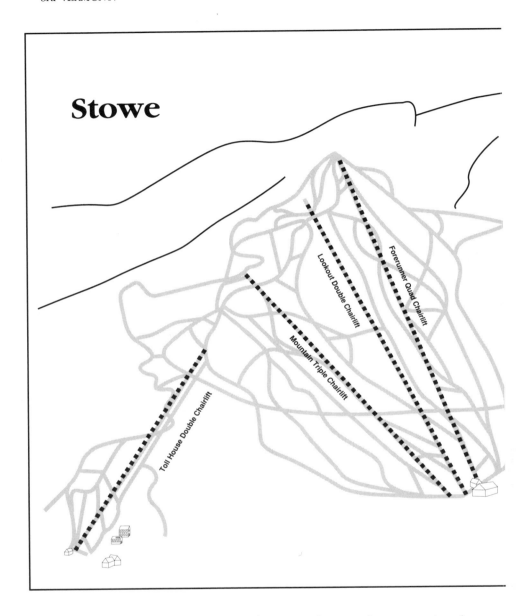

Street and Meadows are Spruce's learning slopes. After mastering them, skiers graduate to the varied and challenging intermediate runs that begin at the Big Spruce and Little Spruce summits. When they're ready for sterner stuff, they pick up the shuttle and head over to Mansfield.

The shuttle is run by the Mt. Mansfield Company, an outfit that is big,

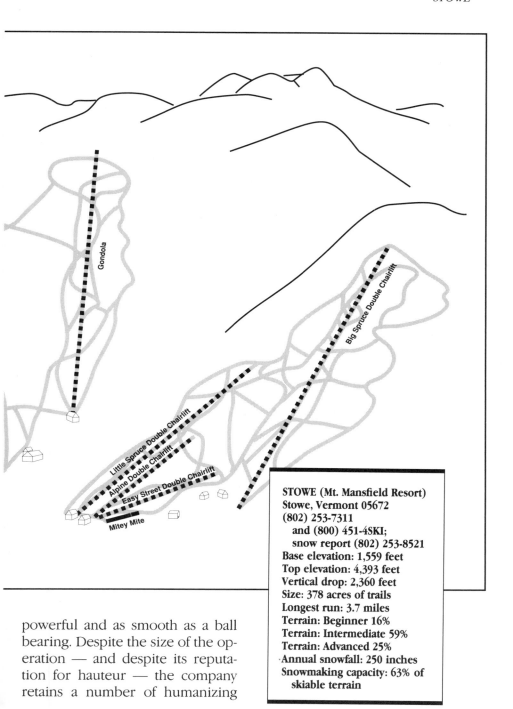

Gondola

Big Spruce Double Chairlift

Little Spruce Double Chairlift

Alpine Double Chairlift

Easy Street Double Chairlift

Mitey Mite

STOWE (Mt. Mansfield Resort)
Stowe, Vermont 05672
(802) 253-7311
  and (800) 451-4SKI;
  snow report (802) 253-8521
Base elevation: 1,559 feet
Top elevation: 4,393 feet
Vertical drop: 2,360 feet
Size: 378 acres of trails
Longest run: 3.7 miles
Terrain: Beginner 16%
Terrain: Intermediate 59%
Terrain: Advanced 25%
Annual snowfall: 250 inches
Snowmaking capacity: 63% of
  skiable terrain

powerful and as smooth as a ball bearing. Despite the size of the operation — and despite its reputation for hauteur — the company retains a number of humanizing touches. Boxes of tissues await the skier at the bottom of the lift, and bagels and lox are available at the restaurant on top.

The newest lift at Mansfield is the Forerunner detachable quadruple chair, a lift whose 1986 debut, like the debut of the original single chair that it replaced, was marked by mechanical problems. Now that they've been worked out, the quad is a high-speed treat. It picks up passengers at a crawling pace, whips them up the mountain, and, at the top, eases them gently back onto the snow. The result is a seven-minute ride that roughly halves the time of a conventional chair.

What happened to the 1940 chairlift? Most of the single seats have been sold to collectors at $300 apiece.

After skiing Mansfield and Spruce, it's time to sample some of Stowe's famous nightlife. It's hard to know where to begin. The region is filled with festivals, first-class hotels, fashionable shops and fine restaurants. Hungry for Italian food? You have a choice of four restaurants. English? Two. Mexican? They've got one. Continental? Try Isle de France, Villa Tragara, Topnotch, Foxfire, Stowehof, Swiss Pot, Ten Acres Lodge — if you don't like the food in Stowe, send your taste buds in for realignment.

Maybe you want to feed the family on something they know and love. On the Mountain Road, Stowe has what must be the most discreet McDonald's in the country. You need a sharp eye to spot the tiny golden arches.

Or maybe you'd like to shop while you're in the area. You won't find discount houses or factory outlets in Stowe. What you will find are some of the best sweater, knitwear and skiwear shops in the world. Many of them, such as Dia's North of Boston, Briscoes and the Moriarity Hat Company, create their own designs.

Like antiques? There are more than 15 stores between Route 15 and I-89, and dozens more on surrounding roads.

Wanna' dance? The Rusty Nail has live bands, and B.K. Clark's alternates between bands and disc jockeys. The Matterhorn starts swinging as soon as the lifts close down. At the Town and Country, Rock King's piano comedy routine keeps 'em tapping and laughing.

Fancy a drink? The Whip is where locals plot their next land deal, The Pub and Mr. Pickwicks are both English pubs, and the Stoweaway is the place to meet your ski instructor off-duty. The Broken Ski Tavern has free hors d'oeuvres and quiet live music.

Sweet tooth? McCarthy's serves coffee and homemade pie to residents and visitors alike, Percy's sells maple syrup and candy, and down the road in Waterbury you've got Green Mountain Chocolates, Cold Hollow

Cider Mill and Ben and Jerry's ice-cream factory!

In case you're concerned about calories, one afternoon of cross-country skiing will trim off any pounds you've put on. Stowe has four major trail systems: In addition to the Mount Mansfield Touring Center there's Edson Hill Manor, Topnotch-at-Stowe and, the most famous of all, the Trapp Family Lodge, whose own extensive trail network connects to the Mansfield touring center.

Since "The Sound of Music" it would be hard to find a country backward enough, a tribe remote enough, a hermit isolated enough not to be able to hum "Doe, a deer, a female deer . . ." along with the Trapps. Their 1938 escape from Nazism is one of the best-known and best-loved family adventures in history.

After fleeing Nazi-controlled Austria, the Trapps recreated themselves as the Trapp Family Singers and toured the United States on the concert circuit. In 1941 they bought a farm in Stowe, and when they eventually gave up professional singing turned their chalet into an inexpensive lodge. Then, just before Christmas, 1980, the lodge burned to the ground, and once again the Trapps re-created themselves. Today the Trapp Family Lodge is nearly as big an attraction as the mountain. No longer inexpensive, it is famous for its cross-country trails, its Austrian ambiance and its high-calorie desserts.

Stowe is not without problems. Despite the new detachable quad, its uphill capacity hasn't kept up with demand, and long lines form on sunny weekends and holidays at both quad and gondola. Stowe's snowmaking has not expanded as much as many of its competitors. And Mt. Mansfield's management has a lingering reputation for arrogance that has driven some skiers to more user-friendly mountains. These factors have limited Stowe's growth and allowed other resorts to surpass it in popularity.

But Stowe has a wonderful, well-cared-for mountain, an extraordinary range of trails, eye-filling views and half a century of skiing tradition. And in the spring of 1991 the resort proposed a multimillion-dollar expansion that would include a new gondola, increased snowmaking capacity, and renovation of its day care center.

• • • • • • • • • • • • • • • • • •

STOWE has some significant challengers for the title of "Ski Capital of the East," but capital or not, it remains a powerful force in the world of skiing. It is a large area with a mighty mountain, rich traditions and an extensive network of alpine and cross-country trails. It's expensive both midweek and weekend but offers several money-saving ski week packages, and with Jay Peak, Bolton, Sugarbush, Mad River and Smugglers' Notch is part of Ski Vermont's Classics. Ask for details.

TIP: Before heading up the mountain, talk to with one of the more than 50 Stowe Hosts. They know where it snowed last night and when individual trails were groomed. Also be sure to take advantage of the free Stowe Host Guided Mountain Tour. Hosts know where to go, and they really know how to ski the mountain.

Another tip: Even when half-hour lines form at the bottom of the quad and the gondola, most other lifts are under-used. So don't go to the back of the queue — skate over to another chairlift. Spend your precious time skiing Stowe, not waiting for a ride up the mountain.

KIDS: At Stowe, Kanga's Pocket looks after up to 40 children from infancy to 3 years; Pooh's Corner involves up to fifty-five 3- to 12-year-olds in arts, crafts and skiing. Both are at Spruce Peak. Graduates of Pooh's Corner can go on to the Mountain Adventure Workshop, a ski school for kids up to 17.

WHERE: Mt. Mansfield Resort is on Route 108 just north of the village of Stowe in the north-central part of the state.

Chapter 15
Stratton Mountain
Upscale, from Top to Bottom

Stratton Mountain is not your average ski area.

The differences start before you've even parked the car. Either you'll be directed into the four-story underground garage or to one of eight parking lots circling the resort. Let's say it's a Saturday and you've been relegated to one of the more distant lots. Just as you're girding your loins for a long hike to the base lodge, a big white school bus pulls up, you climb aboard, and you're whisked to the entrance to Stratton Mountain Village.

The village is the second difference. It's a miniature town built right at the base of the ski lifts. It comes complete with restaurants, deli, bank, jeweler, photo shop, furniture store, several clothing emporiums, and, of course, a clock tower. What's a ski resort without a clock tower?

The third thing you'll notice at Stratton is that the ski-toting shoppers look different from residents of most other villages or even most other ski resorts. They look pampered. The kids all wear braces on their teeth and fur boots on their feet. The adults are decked out in fur and little Bogner numbers that carry four-figure price tags.

You won't notice the fourth difference until you're on the mountain. As you gaze up the slope you'll see more snowboards here than anywhere else in the country. There's a reason for that. Snowboarding began at Stratton. It's Jake Burton Carpenter's home hill. His company, Burton Snowboards — the world's biggest manufacturer and distributor of snowboards — is just down the road in Manchester Center.

For the fifth and final difference, look up. Those futuristic bubbles silently winging their way toward the peak are part of Starship XII, the only 12-passenger gondola in the United States and the newest in North America. It carries 2,400 passengers per hour from base lodge to summit in just seven and a half minutes.

Together, these differences tell a lot about Stratton. Let's look at them one by one:

First, the parking. Stratton has committed itself to making parking lots disappear from slopeside. That's why they've built that multi-level underground garage and why the other lots have been moved away from the base-lodge area. That fleet of white school buses seems always to be there when you want them.

Next, the village. Admittedly, it is something of a shock to see this instant town, a mixture of Kitzbühel and Main Street, USA, appear at the end of a mountain access road in southern Vermont. It's been called "Instant Village" and "Town in a Can," and indeed the whole project, built in the late 1980s, took just three years — and $75 million — to complete.

But consider its virtues. Because all 30 shops and restaurants are clustered tightly together, Stratton has avoided the strip development of other access roads, notably Killington's. By having its housing as well as retail and service sectors ringing the base of the ski slopes, Stratton has avoided the trailside clutter of other areas, notably Okemo.

And the place is kind of cute. Seeing a traditional Vermont bank (OK, what looks like the Hollywood rendition of a traditional Vermont bank) halfway up a mountain, with ski racks instead of parking spaces out front, is a treat for the eyes. Having a choice of eateries and shops within walking distance of your lodgings is a treat for the feet. Noticing that people live above the store (admittedly, above some especially nice stores and in better than the usual above-store conditions) is somehow charming.

About that pampered look. Since its beginnings in 1960, Stratton has had the reputation of catering to what, in pre-Yuppie days, was referred to as wealthy suburbanites. It's an expensive area, and its clientele has expensive tastes.

Snowboards. They cruise, float, fly, boogie, shred and occasionally crash down Stratton's slopes, yet they're no more a hazard to skiers than other skiers. True, they take some getting used to. So did telemarkers. So did chairlifts. True, some complain that snowboarders cut square moguls in the snow. But, like round moguls, they're just another challenge to be mastered on the long and winding trail that leads to the distant, misty kingdom called Masterful Skiing.

How important is Stratton Mountain in the young history of snowboarding? Well, Jake Carpenter tested prototype boards while working as a Stratton bartender. His modus operandi was to sneak his experimental models up on the slopes at night. After Jake left bartending and midnight testing for bigger things, Stratton initiated the snowboard certification program. Today, in addition to its ski school, it runs a flourishing snowboard school with its own headquarters and instructors.

Finally, the gondola. Though sometimes subject to wind interference, it is a genuine honey. Surely the most efficient (and at $3.5 million, the most expensive) gondola in the country, it replaces two old, cold tandem chairlifts that took more than 20 minutes to carry skiers to the summit. While some worried that Starship would send so many people up that there would be traffic jams on the way down, Stratton has mitigated the problem by creating a series of broad trails coming off the top.

Right under Starship is Upper Standard, a wide, gently mogulled trail generously labeled Most Difficult. It runs into Lower Standard, a beginner's slope labeled More Difficult. On days when machine-made snow is all there is, Standard — along with Tamarack and Suntanner — are the best ways down the mountain.

In fact, snowmaking is not Stratton's forte. Officially, 60 percent of the hill is covered, but during snowless seasons it can be a surprisingly icy place. The problem may be in the way the mountain lies to sun and wind or may stem from trying to spread snowmaking over too many trails at the same time. Whatever the cause, it's not from lack of trying; Stratton has the latest snowmaking and snow-grooming equipment and experienced operators running both. That's why the ice is such a surprise.

A second surprise is that Stratton is another top-of-the-market mountain that decorates its slopes with advertising signs. Although they make some effort to keep them in check — they don't sell cigarettes as Magic does — skiers wanting to read Stratton's standing trail maps have to read chewing gum ads on the same sign.

Stratton's trails are divided into three areas: the main hill, Snow Bowl and Sun Bowl. Snow Bowl is on the western side of the mountain, which in inclement weather picks up every bit of wind whipping in from New York State. But when the sun is shining, the view of Bromley's south-facing slopes is gorgeous, and the gentle meadow skiing a delight.

On the southeast side of Stratton is Sun Bowl, the warmest place on the mountain outside the ski lodge. It's the home of Sunriser Supertrail, the widest trail at Stratton and in the state of Vermont. Despite its great expanse (700 feet at its widest point), Sunriser is full of character. Un-

Stratton

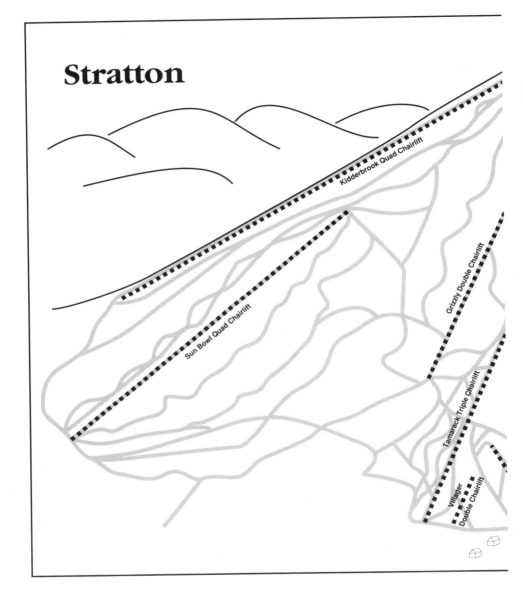

expected dips and hills, islands of trees, quirky side slopes — it's a trail a family of widely differing skiing abilities can enjoy together.

The Sun Bowl also has its share of relatively narrow, relatively easy

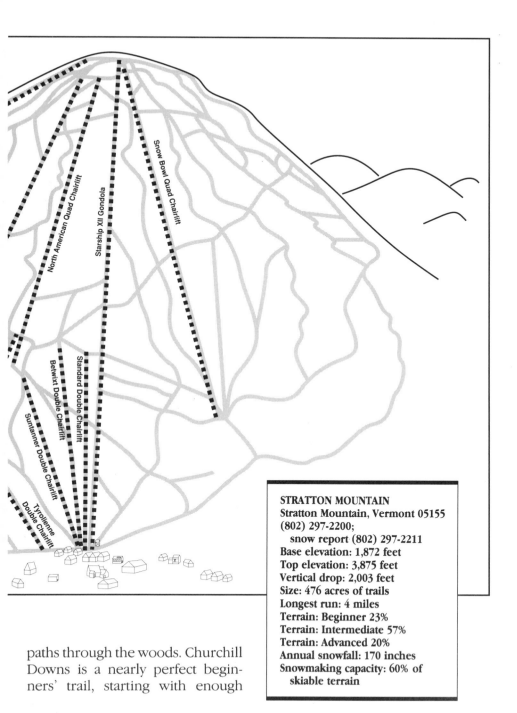

STRATTON MOUNTAIN
Stratton Mountain, Vermont 05155
(802) 297-2200;
   snow report (802) 297-2211
Base elevation: 1,872 feet
Top elevation: 3,875 feet
Vertical drop: 2,003 feet
Size: 476 acres of trails
Longest run: 4 miles
Terrain: Beginner 23%
Terrain: Intermediate 57%
Terrain: Advanced 20%
Annual snowfall: 170 inches
Snowmaking capacity: 60% of
   skiable terrain

paths through the woods. Churchill Downs is a nearly perfect beginners' trail, starting with enough steepness and narrowness to get the heavy breathing going, and ending — like most of the trails on the mountain — with an extended run-out. The Sun Bowl's newest trails, Bear Down and Free Fall, are for experts and are reached by a high-speed quad.

You can easily get to Sun Bowl by skiing down from the top of the mountain, but the alternative is even better. Ski from the Number Eight Chair along the trail named 91/Wanderer. What a treat! More than four miles of skating, cruising, and sometimes briefly climbing along a path

through a forest. Here you are at one of the most popular ski areas in the East, and you find yourself alone in the woods, sharing the experience with only an occasional gray squirrel.

Some skiers get upset with the idea of level locomotion, and even worse, uphill ambulation. But they're among the quiet pleasures of the sport and they're great practice as well. Skating on skis develops balance and teaches you more about weight-change than a dozen wedge-turn runs. Climbing warms you up and builds fabulous thigh muscles. Slow cruising lets you experiment and play.

On the subject of play, you can get a lot of après-ski time in at Stratton without ever leaving the mountain. There's usually a band playing at Café Applause, downstairs at the Stratton Mountain Inn. The famous Stratton Mountain Boys play their oom-pah music in the Bear's Den at the base lodge. And there's daily après-ski entertainment at Mulligan's in the Village Square.

For food, you have eight choices of restaurants plus a rather expensive cafeteria, all on the mountain. La Pizzeria, specializing in guess what, is the newest place in the village. Mulligan's is the hottest, drawing big crowds for lunching, dinnering and pubbing. Sage Hill is more formal, and many consider Birkenhaus one of the best restaurants in the area.

. . . .

STRATTON is an upmarket place, a shopper's Shangri-la capped by a dream gondola lift. The skiing is mainly beginner and intermediate on a hill big enough to give a week's worth of variety. There's a 2,003-foot vertical drop, a summit elevation of 3,875 feet and 12 lifts including the gondola. Food, lodging and accessories are on the expensive side; lift tickets are pricey.

TIP: When skiing Stratton, drive to the Sun Bowl lodge. Purchase your lift ticket there and avoid the majority of skiers, who gravitate toward the base lodge. From the Sun Bowl you can ski the entire mountain.

KIDS: Like most Vermont ski areas, Stratton names its children's programs after bears. I don't know why. There's the Little Cub Ski School for ages 4 to 6, and the Big Cub for kids 7 to 12. Both provide morning and afternoon lessons, supervised playtime and lunch. Both are affiliated with SKIwee. There's also a large child care center accommodating children from 6 weeks to 5 years. A child who is 12 or under gets free tickets if an accompanying adult buys non-holiday tickets for three days or more. Kids 6 and under ski free.

WHERE: Stratton Mountain Road starts off Route 30 in southern Vermont, about 15 miles east of Manchester.

Chapter 16

Sugarbush

Two Big Mountains and a Beautiful Valley

Sugarbush the word is pure country Vermont. When a farmer points to the stand of maples that he taps each spring to make maple syrup, he says, "That's my sugarbush."

Sugarbush the resort is anything but country Vermont. You don't get the nickname "Mascara Mountain" from wearing plaid wool shirts and saying "Ay-yup."

Sugarbush was founded by New York glitterati for the use of their friends and a few other well-heeled skiers who might care to drop by. Those who did drop by included most of the Kennedy clan (including daredevil skier, now senator, Ted); fashion designer Oleg Cassini; his brother, gossip-columnist Igor Cassini a/k/a Cholly Knickerbocker; bandleader Skitch Henderson; restaurateur Armando Orsini; and half the leading models in New York. The models provided the mascara in the nickname.

Along with a couple of Heinz and Avon heirs, a Greek shipping magnate, a banker and a countess or two, these trendsetters turned Sugarbush into their own American St. Moritz.

Between them, they made Sugarbush *the* place to ski in the East. Cassini's only regret was that he didn't have the foresight to buy 7,000 acres of nearby land — he didn't want to pay the asking price of $7 an acre.

These jet-setting years were the early 1960s, shortly after Sugarbush was founded by socialites Damon and Sara Gadd and their friend Jack Murphy. After scouring the East, the Gadds say they chose the Mad River Valley because they found a big mountain (3,975-foot Lincoln Peak) with a heavy (250 inches) annual snowfall. No doubt this played a big part. But they must have been swayed by the beauty of the region.

Even in Vermont, where scenic beauty usually lies just outside the dooryard, the Mad River Valley is special. Tall, broad-shouldered mountains arch out of narrow valleys. From the ridge tops, the view takes in half of northern New England. That's Lake Champlain to the west, Mt. Washington to the east, and Mad River Glen just over the next rise. The two closest towns, Waitsfield and Warren, are handsome, and manage to combine an old-fashioned Vermont feel with the unmistakable air of prosperity. Gliders soar high above the valley all summer, and skiers slide down the surrounding peaks from November through April. No wonder the owners and their jet-setting friends were drawn here. No wonder it became *the* place to ski.

Besides the Beautiful People, Sugarbush had something else that made it unique in its early years: the world's longest gondola, a string of colorful, three-passenger bubbles dangling from a cable that carried warm — if somewhat cramped — customers 9,300 feet in 15 minutes.

Today, except for one remaining bubble car permanently parked inside the Valley House base lodge, the gondola is gone, replaced in 1984 by the Sugar Bravo and Heaven's Gate triple chairs.

Why trade a gondola for a couple of chairlifts? Two reasons. Gondolas — particularly early ones — were at the mercy of the wind and often had to be shut down in a stiff breeze. And even when running at full capacity, the bubble cars could only haul 450 skiers per hour to the peak. The two triple chairs carry 1,800 skiers, wind or no wind.

Now into its third decade, Sugarbush has changed hands four times and changed management many times more. Most of the jet set have gone the way of the gondola. But they left a permanent stamp on the resort and on the region.

Part of their legacy can be seen in the myriad luxury homes, chalets and condos tucked discreetly into wooded lots on the approach roads and throughout the surrounding countryside.

Another part of the jet set legacy is in the richness of the services that spread like a fan pointed east from the base of Mt. Lincoln. Restaurants, inns, hotels, bed and breakfasts — all are here in great quantity and almost startling quality.

Getting onto the mountain at Sugarbush starts with choosing which mountain you want to get onto. In 1979 the owners bought their nearest neighbor, Glen Ellen Ski Area. They changed the name to Sugarbush North, then to Mount Ellen, which was its name to start with, and then back to Sugarbush North. There are long-range plans to connect this peak with Sugarbush South, formerly South Basin, originally Sugarbush. But for now, all they share is a lift ticket. So you have to choose which mountain to head for.

One reason to choose North over South is that it has more snow-making capacity — 66 percent compared with 38 percent. Another is that it has steeper trails — in fact, some of the steepest in the East. A third is that it's got a bit more elevation — 4,083 feet to South's 3,975 feet.

Three new quads (one of them the world's fastest chairlift), two double chairs and two surface lifts serve Sugarbush North, and although the number of trails is somewhat limited, they offer skiing for a broad range of skill levels. At the top skill level are Upper FIS, a broad chute plummeting down from the summit, and the aptly named Exterminator, a narrow alley nearly as steep as FIS.

But you needn't be an expert to ski the top. Rim Run is a lovely, winding intermediate trail from the peak that feeds into the long, straight, gentle Northway before dropping into the intermediate (though sometimes bumpy) Which Way, Cruiser and North Star. Which Way is the trail of choice when natural snow is sparse.

Cross-country skiers are sometimes seen making their way along the ridgeline. They're on Vermont's famous Long Trail, which runs the length of the ridge on its way between Canada and Massachusetts.

If Sugarbush South is neither so high nor so snow-enhanced as its northern sibling, it offers greater breadth in both uphill and downhill departments. Sugarbush South has seven chairs and two Poma lifts. The fastest way down is via Organgrinder, a perfectly straight run from the top to mid-mountain. There, it makes a quick detour like a drain trap, then continues straight down the hill. It's not for the weak or inexperienced, and when snow cover is light, it's not for the even marginally sane.

Nearly as long and straight, though not nearly so steep, is Hot Shot, an intermediate trail off the Gate House chair. Real hotshots are going to be happier taking the Castlerock chair, which begins halfway up the mountain and empties onto exclusively expert trails. Among the most notable are Liftline, Rumble and Middle Earth.

The best known trail at Sugarbush is Jester, a surprise-filled, high-intermediate course that wanders down from the peak, twisting, turning and reversing on itself as it makes its eccentric way toward the base lodge. Jester is one of the original trails at Sugarbush, and today it remains

Sugarbush

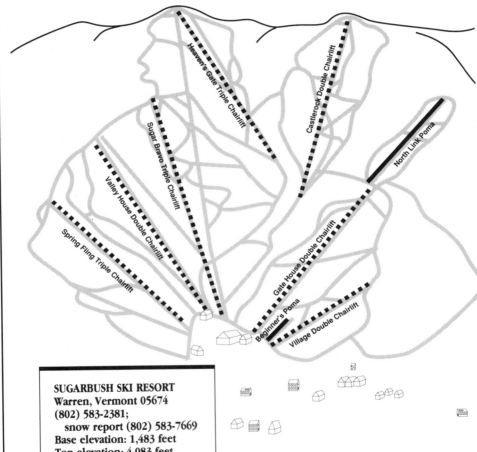

SUGARBUSH SKI RESORT
Warren, Vermont 05674
(802) 583-2381;
    snow report (802) 583-7669
Base elevation: 1,483 feet
Top elevation: 4,083 feet
Vertical drop: 2,600 feet
Size: 380 acres of trails
Longest run: 2.5 miles
Terrain: Beginner 15%
Terrain: Intermediate 44%
Terrain: Advanced 41%
Annual snowfall: 252 inches
Snowmaking capacity: 45% of
    skiable terrain

one of the outstanding intermediate trails in the country. If a trail can be said to have a sense of humor, Jester has it.

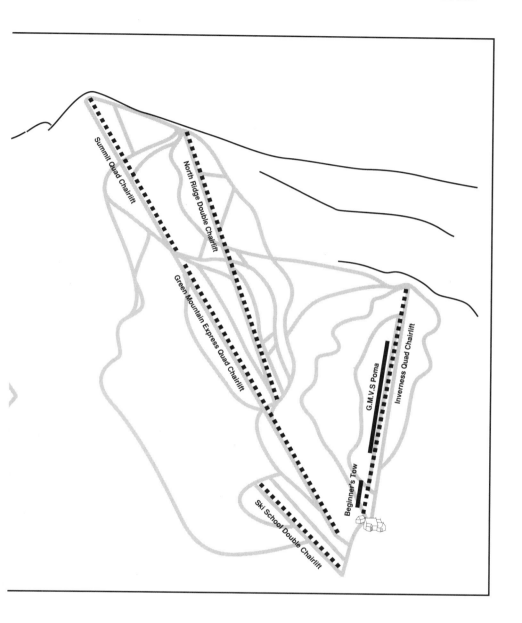

The 1990s brought two out of three badly needed changes to Sugarbush. With three new quads installed in 1990, Sugarbush leapt from a lift system that was barely adequate to one of the most advanced in the country. With its belated discovery that kids need off-snow entertainment, it grew from an adults-only scene to a resort that provides for families as well as swingers.

That's two down and one to go. The next step the area must take is to increase its ability to make snow. When that's in place, this twin-peak resort will be unstoppable.

After skiing, there's still a lot going on around Sugarbush. Start with restaurants. Fancy a French dinner? Chez Henri is famous for them. Creative-eclectic? Sam Rupert's is outstanding. Prime rib? The Bass Tavern is the leading rib house for miles. Mexican? Miguel's serves the best of Green Mountain Mex. Continental? The Common Man. Over-the-top desserts? It's illegal to leave town without having dessert at the Phoenix.

Nightlife in the valley doesn't offer quite the depth of the restaurants, but there's enough to keep most folks happy. Both Chez Henri and the Bass Tavern have discos. The Blue Tooth and Gallaghers feature rock bands. Après-ski (but not après-dinner), Knickers offers mellow music by the blazing fire. Ski movies run on Saturdays at the Gate House. In Waitsfield, first-run flicks are shown and first-rate drinks are poured at Edison's Studio.

Youngsters used to be neglected at Sugarbush, but no more. They can go sledding under lights, enjoy a campfire on Friday nights, and take part in treasure hunts, snow volleyball and snowshoeing. There's Teen Night at the Sports Center every Saturday, with sports facilities and dancing to a d.j.

Lodging in and around the valley runs the gamut from ski dorms with bunk beds to the most elegant bed and breakfast in the state (maybe in the solar system).

Here's a sample. The only full service hotel is the Sugarbush Inn; it has beautiful public rooms, good-but-not-gourmet food. The most upscale condos are in the Southface complex. In Waitsfield, the Valley Inn is a friendly, knotty-pine-ish place on Route 100. Because owner Bill Stinson is a well-known glider instructor, it's the spot to talk soaring. Down the road in Moretown, the Schultz Village Inn has a cozy feel, shared baths, kitchen privileges (in a wonderful kitchen) and among the most reasonable rates in the valley. Book well in advance. Further down the road, the Carpenter Farm is a working farm that manages to accommodate up to 165 skiers by bunking them upper and lower. Rates are mid-range, but negotiable. Back in Waitsfield, but well away from the busy center of town, Beaver Pond Farm is cozy, friendly and right on the golf course. No, there's no golf in winter, but golf courses make ideal cross-country ski terrain.

And then there's the Inn at Round Barn Farm. The inn — OK, bed and breakfast — is a restored historic farm with an attached round — OK, 12-sided — barn, one of only a dozen left in the state. The restoration/redecoration of the house took 18 months, and many more months went into the barn. It was time well spent. Everything, from the antique beds to the wide-board floors, from the in-room Jacuzzis to the exposed beam ceilings, from the warm hospitality to the brilliant breakfasts, is first rate. No pets, no kids, and no smoking.

Sugarbush also has a super sports center, complete with indoor pool, aerobics, Nautilus, Jacuzzi, steam room and sauna, as well as tennis, squash and raquetball courts.

• • • • • • • • • • • • • • • • •

SUGARBUSH'S greatest strengths are a pair of big, varied, challenging mountains set in a valley of extraordinary beauty and filled with fine restaurants, inns and private homes.

TIPS: Sugarbush South is a broad, steep bowl. Sun and snow conditions often differ widely from one part of the bowl to another. The trails on either end may be bathed in sunlight while the middle is as dark as a fogbound forest. Look for the sun and ask other skiers (or the ski patrol) where conditions are best.

If you're looking for lessons that are out of the ordinary, consider the Centered Skiing Workshops at the Sugarbush Ski School. They're designed for advanced skiers mired in a rut or stuck on a plateau. Their focus is on getting mind and body to operate together. They're serious and playful, hard and soft, earthy and ethereal. And they work.

KIDS: Sugarbush Day School takes children from 6 weeks to 2 years and entertains them with music, crafts, stories and outdoor activities. The Minibear program is for 4- and 5-year-olds. It's an indoor-outdoor session for beginning skiers, naps included. The Sugarbear program lets 6- to 10-year-olds learn on Mogul Mouseland, a fantasy terrain garden with bumps, turns and tunnels.

WHERE: The turn for Sugarbush is off Route 100 in central Vermont, about 3 miles north of Warren, 4 miles south of Waitsfield and 20 miles south of Montpelier.

Chapter 17

On The Small Side

By Mark Pendergrast

Do good things really come in small packages? Vermont's community ski areas offer contemporary proof of that old adage. At the state's smallest ski areas, vertical drop is usually measured in hundreds of feet, not thousands. Skiers who want truly big mountains and cosmopolitan after-ski nightlife will still seek out the major resorts, but a quieter, more informal type of skiing is alive and well throughout Vermont.

It can be found at Northeast Slopes in East Corinth, where a rope tow powered by a 1960 farm truck will put a bit of strain on your shoulder but hardly a dent in your wallet. Modeled after the historic ski tow that inaugurated downhill skiing in Woodstock in 1934, this one has been running in its present location since 1936. That makes Northeast Slopes the oldest functioning rope tow hill in existence.

At the other end of the technological scale, community skiing can also be found at Suicide Six, where a modern double chairlift whisks skiers up The Face, the near-vertical mountainside just north of Woodstock that looms over an extensive base lodge, bar, and restaurant.

It can also be found at Prospect Mountain in Bennington, where cross-country trails through the woods augment the downhill slopes. Or at the Middlebury Snow Bowl, where local college students bomb down the slopes and there's a library in the base lodge.

These and other small ski areas are appealing because of their informality, inexpensive lift tickets, and sense of old-fashioned fun. Many of the skiers are local people who bring their children. Volunteers often staff the snack bar and lifts.

A call to confirm conditions, prices, and times of operation is recommended before visiting.

MIDDLEBURY COLLEGE SNOW BOWL, *Ripton*

The Middlebury College Snow Bowl, located in Robert Frost country in Ripton, just east of Middlebury, has more varied terrain and a greater choice of runs on its 20 miles of trails than most other small areas. The

Snow Bowl is not, in fact, very small. Its 1,200-foot vertical drop is impressive. It boasts three different lifts, an active ski school, and 30 miles of groomed cross-country trails just down the road at the Rikert Touring Center on the Breadloaf Campus.

What makes Middlebury primarily a family ski center isn't its size or its price, but its location and ambiance. As Howard Kelton, the general manager, puts it, "We have no bar. We don't advertise. There is not much housing available nearby. In fact, you can't see a condo or even a rooftop from the top of the mountain."

Instead of a bar, the Snow Bowl has a library — perhaps the only ski area in the state that does — where studies mix comfortably with sport. Kelton admits, though, that snowmaking, not books, is what lures so many Middlebury students to the slopes.

For the greatest choice, take the 4,200-foot Worth Mountain chairlift. From the top, you can either take a long swing back to the lodge on the intermediate Proctor trail or zip down the expert Allen or Ross trails. Or, take the Youngman over to the base of the Bailey Falls triple chairlift for a ride up the east slope. Or take Voter, a beginner trail, down to the Sheehan chairlift for yet more choices. Wherever you go, the views will be breathtaking. From one point on the Youngman trail, you can see the Adirondacks, Lake Champlain, and Pico Peak.

Fees and passes at the Snow Bowl are moderate in price. Rates for children and seniors vary, but if you're over 70, you ski for free. And there are quite a few skiers in that category, according to ski school director Dwight Dunning, who personally teaches a group whose ages range from 66 to 78. The area also sponsors a racing program and has produced many college racers and Olympic skiers, some of whom stop by the area and help out.

The Snow Bowl is open daily from 9 a.m. to 4 p.m., weather permitting. A full range of ski rentals is available, as is wholesome food at a reasonable price. For more information, call (802) 388-4356.

SUICIDE SIX, *Pomfret*

Despite the dramatic name, even novice skiers can enjoy themselves at this historic ski area. Bunny Bertram, who began the area in 1937 when he moved it from nearby Gilbert's Hill, site of the first U.S. ski tow, was looking for a catchy name. "It was Hill number 6 on the topographical map, and I remembered my alliteration from English class so I called it Suicide Six," Bertram said.

At 650 feet, the vertical drop isn't overwhelming. But it is awe inspiring as you look at The Face, the sheer slope directly behind the base lodge. The broad slope allows ample room for turning, though, and you don't have to be a professional skier to enjoy the moguls.

There are two double chairlifts that provide plenty of runs per day for avid skiers. The 2,000-foot lift takes you to the top of The Face or Show Off, both expert trails. You can also swing down Easy Mile for a gentler run or, for intermediates, Bunny's Boulevard. Or, scoot down The Gully and through Back Door, both intermediate trails, where the Milky Way is the easiest way down. The Lift Line itself is only an intermediate run, provided you avoid the poles on your way down. A 400-foot beginners' T-bar is just $3 all day, and offers the perfect spot for novices of all ages.

Because Suicide Six is owned by the Woodstock Inn & Resort, visitors can take advantage of numerous other amenities. The Woodstock Ski Touring Center is just down the road, as is the Woodstock Sports Center, featuring racquetball, tennis, weight training, and an indoor pool. If you stay any night, Sunday through Thursday, at the Woodstock Inn & Resort, you get free skiing at Suicide Six and the ski touring center, plus free rentals and use of the sports center.

Suicide Six offers the advantages of a larger area, including ski school, rentals, cafeteria, and a bar/lounge. The base lodge is airy, with lots of windows and deck space to view the action on the slopes. But this ski area is still small enough so that families can ski together or separately without fear of getting lost.

Day tickets, season passes, and single-ride tickets are moderate in price. The slopes are open daily from 9 a.m. to 4 p.m. There is snowmaking on more than half the runs.

For more information, call (802) 457-1666.

NORWICH UNIVERSITY, *Northfield*

It isn't hard to identify the cadets who constitute about half the skiers at the Norwich University Ski Area in Northfield. Not only do they sport military haircuts, but when you speak to them they are invariably polite. Yes sir, No, ma'am. They're also unusually good skiers, since using the slopes costs them nothing. It's part of the tuition, and the ski area is within 300 yards of the dorms. That accounts, in part, for the fact that of a total student body of 1,300, roughly 800 students per week ski there.

Only in part, though — because the 902-foot vertical drop, carved from Paine Mountain in 1970, offers a thrilling variety of skiing, short lift lines, and reasonable rates. That's why Montpelier residents, only 15 minutes away, often use the area. So do groups from Massachusetts and beyond. Special group rates are available for clubs of 10 or more through advance notice only.

There is a 300-foot Mighty Mite tow in the "Kinder Bowl" for youngsters and beginners. On the main slope, a 3,700-foot double chair lift rushes skiers to the top, where they can use the free guide maps or look at the trail poster at the summit to plan their runs. G.S. and Lybrand are expert trails, Tally-Ho and Stagecoach are relatively gentle runs, and Bull Run and Down Hill are for intermediates.

There is a six-mile cross-country system beginning to the left of the liftline. Lazier cross-country skiers can pay $2 and take the lift up for a head start. There is a warming hut, snack bar, ski shop, and rental area, and ski lessons are offered at group, semi-private, and private rates.

The area is open 10 a.m. to 4 p.m. on weekends and holiday weeks, and 12:30 p.m. to 4 p.m. weekdays. Prices are moderate. For snow conditions, call (802) 485-2155.

COCHRAN'S, *Richmond*

Mickey and Ginny Cochran have parented one of the most famous skiing clans in the world. Between 1969 and 1976, their four children — Marilyn, Barbara Ann, Bobby, and Lindy — took a total of 12 U.S. national championships in downhill, slalom, and giant slalom. In 1972, Barbara Ann won the Olympic gold medal in the slalom in Sapporo, Japan.

All four children and many other premier U.S. skiers trained on a relatively small hill in Richmond, where Cochran's Ski Area still offers what Ginny calls "the last ma-and-pa ski area in Vermont."

The Cochrans put in a 400-foot rope tow behind their house in 1961 to give their kids a place to practice skiing after school. In 1974, after a year as the U.S. alpine ski coach and a brief return to his engineering job at General Electric, Mickey Cochran "retired" to devote his energies to promoting and maintaining the ski area, which now has a 1,600-foot T-bar, a 1,100-foot rope tow, and 450-foot Mighty Mite beginner's tow in addition to the original tow.

Skiers originally trooped through the Cochran kitchen for hot chocolate but can now enjoy goodies and relaxation in a recently completed lodge (the only building that still has a mortgage, Mickey proudly notes).

The Cochran Ski Club, officially a separate entity from the ski area, gives kids the same shot at ski racing that the Cochran offspring had. Although he takes no official part in coaching, Mickey frequently views videotapes of young skiers and makes helpful comments. He also has a library of Olympic videos that the skiers repeatedly ask to see.

The Cochran children remain involved to one degree or another in the ski area. Lindy, who lives nearby in Starksboro, coaches in the ski club program. Barbara Ann, who teaches in Barre, frequently comes to help on weekends. Bobby, now a doctor in New Hampshire, also helps when he can. Even Marilyn, who lives in Switzerland, helps out when she's visiting.

The area offers snowmaking on "I-89," one of the more difficult trails, and the short Mighty Mite trail. Lollipop Races are held every Sunday. Begun years ago, they offer low-key slalom experience to children. All who finish get a lollipop.

Cochran's is open daily except Mondays and Wednesdays. On weekdays, the hours are 2:30 p.m. to 5 p.m.; on weekends, 9:30 a.m. to 4 p.m. Ginny Cochran offers ski lessons at 10 a.m. on weekends.

Lift ticket prices are relatively inexpensive. For more information, call the Cochrans at (802) 434-2479.

MAPLE VALLEY, *West Dummerston*

Maple Valley prides itself on being a family ski area. Located less than a half hour from Massachusetts, it has 17 trails, a recently added third floor on its large, modern lodge and two refurbished double chairlifts. Most significantly, though, it has 100 percent snowmaking capability on the mountain, which has a 1,000-foot vertical drop.

Maple Valley caters to families with small children who are just entering the sport of skiing. The area offers "First-Time Skier" packages for young and old alike. It provides some of the amenities of a larger ski area, such as a lounge area in the base lodge and a complete retail ski shop, but still boasts many small ski area traits. The cafeteria opens early each morning with made-to-order breakfasts, and continues throughout the day and night with homemade soups, sandwiches and salads.

The area has a ski school and hosts the Maple Valley Racing Academy, a program for 8- to 15-year-olds; NASTAR races, and more than 20 after-school learn-to-ski programs for area children.

About half its skiers are local, the remainder from neighboring states. They come for the comfortable, relaxed atmosphere, convenient accommodations in nearby Putney, Brattleboro, and Newfane and, of course, for the skiing, which ranges from a beginners' T-bar to Stormin' Norman, a favorite expert slope. Guando Bear is a long, easy run that winds down from the top of the mountain.

Prices at Maple Valley are moderate to inexpensive, and there is night skiing on some trails (until 10 p.m., 11 p.m. on holidays). For more information, call (802) 254-6083.

PROSPECT MOUNTAIN SKI AREA, *Woodford*

Prospect Mountain Ski Area, on Route 9 in Woodford between Bennington and Wilmington, offers a substantial vertical drop (700 feet), warm west-facing slopes, and one of the best-maintained cross-country trail networks in southern Vermont.

Begun in 1939 as a local rope tow, the area blossomed in 1960 when the highway from Bennington was widened to three lanes. Bennington contractor William H. Morse bought the ski area and, using his company's equipment, built the parking lot, made new trails, and put in the major T-bar. For almost 20 years, Morse ran the area.

In 1979, sick of routine real estate transactions and endless title searches, Bennington lawyer Joe Parks bought Prospect Mountain and has only occasionally regretted his action. "I've chosen to keep the downhill as it is and to develop the cross-country aspect more seriously," Parks says. "I could put another $1.5 million into the area, put in snowmaking, lights, a double chairlift, and a modern lodge, but I still couldn't compete with the major mountains for vertical drop."

Parks' decision to remain a smaller, more informal area, with an older, patched-up base lodge, should suit families in search of a casual atmosphere with varied terrain and excellent skiing.

Beginners can start on the small rope tow, run out of a 1930 International truck parked backwards. Others can advance to the smaller T-bar, which goes a third of the way up the slope, or to the 3,000-foot-long T-bar, which gives a choice of four main downhill trails, a mile or more in length, all named for some aspect of the Battle of Bennington. Beginners will want to take the gentle Seth Warner trail. The John Stark is a swooping intermediate, and Cannonball and Yankee Courage are for the experts.

The cross-country trails are open throughout the snow season. On weekends, both alpine and cross-country facilities are open. Every Thursday night through Saturday night, lights are turned on, illuminating a third of the mountain for skiing and snowboarding.

Cross-country and alpine rentals are available, as are snowboarding demonstrations. Prices for rentals, lessons, lifts, and trail fees are all inexpensive to moderate. For information, call (802) 442-2575.

At the area, Buck's Tavern serves homemade chowders, soups, pizzas, and sandwiches on Thursdays, and opens as a regular restaurant with full-course dinners on Fridays and Saturdays.

LYNDON OUTING CLUB, *Lyndonville*

Continuity is the word that describes the Lyndon Outing Club, which celebrated its 50th anniversary in 1987 with sleigh rides, oyster stew, ski races, a torchlight parade and fireworks. The first LOC carnival queen, crowned in 1939, was Harriet Fletcher Fisher, who is still active on the board of directors. Don Beattie, one of the founding members of the club, is also on the board and is one of the most active skiers on the slopes. Both Fisher and Beattie live in the same houses they were raised in. Their grandchildren ski at LOC, too.

The ski club was begun in 1937 by young people who wanted a place to ski after work during the weekdays. LOC is still run almost exclusively by volunteers. Each of the 36 directors takes a turn in the base lodge snack bar, which can be quite active. On a busy weekend, about 500 skiers descend on the area.

Through the years, the Outing Club hosted major college ski competitions and ski jumping meets. Now these are only memories, but the area sponsors ski races for elementary students in droves: more than a hundred show up for weekend races.

Primarily, though, the Lyndon Outing Club offers true family skiing. Lift tickets are inexpensive. Slopes are open on Saturday, 9 a.m. to 5 p.m., and Sunday, noon to 5 p.m. The area is also open from 6:30 to 9:30 p.m. on Tuesday, Wednesday, Friday, and Saturday. The vertical drop is 433 feet.

For more information, call LOC president John Raymond at (802) 626-8465.

NORTHEAST SLOPES, *East Corinth*

Northeast Slopes, a community-run operation, has been providing skiing since 1936. The area boasts that it has one of the longest natural ski seasons in Vermont due to its northeast exposure, which allows less sun to strike the hillside.

Skiers can choose from two tows. A 400-footer for beginners runs directly out of the back seat of a wrecked 1973 Plymouth Valiant. On a cold morning, you'll find John Pierson, who owns the Shell station down the road, jump-starting the engine. The 1,250-foot tow is powered by a 1960 Ford farm truck. A large red "panic button" allows the operator to slow the tow to a crawl instantly if there is a problem.

On a typical day, Northeast Slopes is a very busy place, with an average of 150 skiers of all ages descending its 350-foot vertical drop.

The lifts normally operate from 9 a.m. to 4 p.m. on weekends and school holidays. Lift fees at Northeast Slopes are inexpensive. For more information call Rick Cook at (802) 439-5368 or the area, 439-5789, weekends.

Chapter 18

Skiing Cross-Country

In the past 20 years, cross-country skiing has taken root and flourished in Vermont. Today the state has nearly 50 nordic centers that offer a tremendous variety of skiing, from relaxed back-country touring to smooth, fast traveling over finely groomed trails. Instruction is available at virtually all areas. We've mentioned many of these centers in the course of reviewing the major downhill areas. Here is a complete list, with telephone numbers so you can call for current information on prices and conditions.

NORTH

 1. Bolton Valley Resort, Bolton, 05477. (802) 434-2131.
 2. Burke Mountain, East Burke, 05832. (802) 626-8338.
 3. Camel's Hump Nordic, Huntington, 05462. (802) 434-2704.
 4. Catamount Family Center, Williston, 05495. (802) 879-6001.
 5. Craftsbury Nordic, Craftsbury Common, 05827. (802) 586-7768.
 6. Edson Hill, Stowe, 05672. (802) 253-8954.
 7. Hazen's Notch, Montgomery Center., 05471. (802) 326-4708.
 8. Heermansmith Farm Inn, Coventry, 05825. (802) 754-8866.
 9. Highland Lodge, Greensboro, 05841. (802) 533-2647.
10. Jay Peak, Jay, 05859. (802) 988-2611.
11. Mount Mansfield, Stowe, 05672. (802) 253-7311.
12. Sherman Hollow, Richmond, 05477. (802) 434-2057.
13. Smugglers' Notch, Jeffersonville, 05464. (802) 644-8851.
14. Sterling Ridge Inn, Jeffersonville, 05464. (802) 644-8265.
15. Sugarmill Farm, Barton, 05822. (802) 525-3701.
16. Topnotch, Stowe, 05672. (802) 253-8585.
17. Trapp Family Lodge, Stowe, 05672. (802) 253-8511.
18. Wolf Run, Bakersfield, 05441. (802) 933-4007.

CENTRAL

19. Blueberry Hill, Goshen, 05733. (802) 247-6535.
20. Blueberry Lake, East Warren, 05674. (802) 496-6687.

21. Churchill House, Brandon, 05733. (802) 247-3300.
22. Green Mountain, Randolph, 05060. (802) 728-5575.
23. Green Trails, Brookfield, 05036. (802) 276-3412.
24. Lake Morey Inn, Fairlee, 05045. (802) 333-4800.
25. Mountain Meadows, Killington, 05751. (802) 775-7077.
26. Mountain Top, Chittenden, 05737. (802) 483-6089.
27. Ole's, Warren, 05674. (802) 496-3430.
28. Rikert's, Ripton, 05766. (802) 388-2759.
29. Sugarbush Inn, Warren, 05674. (802) 583-2301.
30. Trail Head, Stockbridge, 05772. (802) 746-8038.
31. Tucker Hill, Waitsfield, 05673. (802) 496-3983.
32. Wilderness Trails, Quechee, 05059. (802) 295-7620.
33. Woodstock, Woodstock, 05091. (802) 457-2114.

SOUTH

34. Ascutney Mountain, Brownsville, 05037. (802) 484-7711.
35. Brattleboro Ski Hut, Brattleboro, 05301. (802) 254-4081.
36. Fox Run, Ludlow, 05149. (802) 228-8871.
37. Grafton Ponds, Grafton, 05146. (802) 843-2231.
38. Hawk, Plymouth, 05056. (802) 672-3811.
39. Hermitage, Wilmington, 05363. (802) 464-3511.
40. Hildene, Manchester, 05254. (802) 362-1788.
41. Nordic Inn, Landgrove, 05148. (802) 824-6444.
42. Prospect Ski Mountain, Woodford, 05201. (802) 442-2575.
43. Sitzmark, Wilmington, 05363. (802) 464-5498.
44. Stratton, Stratton Mt., 05155. (802) 297-1880.
45. Tater Hill, Chester, 05143. (802) 875-2517.
46. Timber Creek, Wilmington, 05363. (802) 464-0999.
47. Viking, Londonderry, 05148. (802) 824-3933.
48. White House, Wilmington, 05363. (802) 464-2135.
49. Wild Wings, Peru, 05152. (802) 824-6793.

Cross-Country Skiing in Vermont

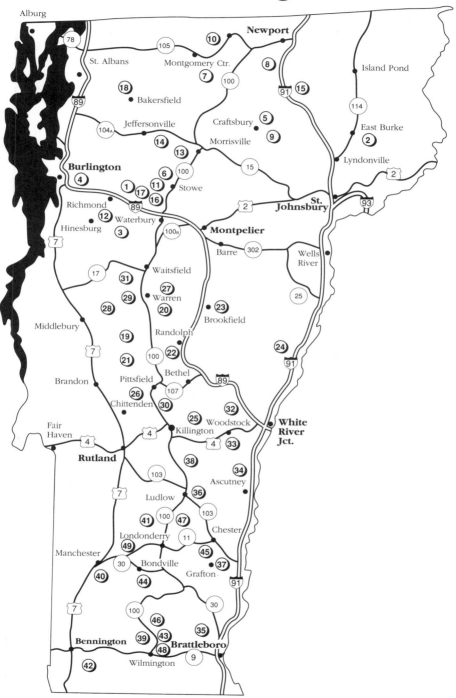

Chapter 19

How to Beat the High Price of Skiing

It comes as something of a shock to find lift-ticket prices are up again.

Of course it was a shock when tickets crossed the $20 mark. People predicted that the sport had priced itself out of existence. They made the same prediction at $25, at $30, at $35. No doubt they'll do the same at $50. Yet, despite the predictions, skiing is still very much alive.

But that doesn't mean you have to pay top dollar to enjoy it. Here's how to avoid the big bite:

The first strategy is to ski midweek. Granted, this option is not available to all, and not available to most on a regular basis. But, as they say, where there's a wedel, there's a way. Those who find that way can reap substantial savings.

How substantial? It varies from mountain to mountain, year to year, but you can safely expect to save at least 30 percent by avoiding weekend and holiday skiing. At the same time, you'll double the quantity and quality of your skiing experience.

The second way to cut costs is to do anything you can to avoid buying a single-day ticket. There is simply no more expensive way to ski than by the day.

The most obvious strategy to avoid paying full-retail is to purchase a season's pass. You can save a bundle this way, but with two caveats: you always have to ski the same area, and you have to ski it a lot.

If you like to flit about during the ski season, or if you ski only when conditions are perfect, a season's pass can end up costing you money.

But there are other alternatives. If you have a block of ski time — say, a week — buy a five-day pass at your favorite hill, then go out and flail those trails. The savings are significant.

Night skiing at Bolton Valley is another way to cut costs. Dress warmly.

Smugglers' Notch sells a Bash Badge that entitles regulars to ski for greatly reduced prices, every day of the season. Sugarbush sells discounted tickets at area banks and supermarkets, enabling you to save money and save a wait in the ticket line at the same time you're stocking up on dog food. Other areas have their own savings plans; ask and they'll be glad to tell you.

If you're staying at a ski resort, all manner of discount plans will be available. If you're staying at a resort with your family, the discounts will be even greater.

Some mountains team up, offering one pass for all. Bromley and Magic Mountain are a pair; Killington and Pico are unequal siblings. (At certain times a Killington ticket will get you into Pico, but not vice versa.) Further north, six resorts — Jay Peak, Bolton Valley, Mad River Glen, Sugarbush, Stowe, and Smugglers' Notch — have formed Ski Vermont's Classics. Classics passholders can mix and match to their heart's content and save money at the same time. But note, some of these mountains are almost an hour's driving time apart.

Another way around the big prices has received surprisingly little press in Vermont. It's simply to be a Vermonter and be able to prove it. Jay Peak and Burke Mountain not only give Vermonters discounts, they give them to Canadians (Jay) and New Hampshirites (Burke) as well. Although not every area gives credit for in-state status, many do. Ask.

Another savings plan is to use your age. If you're lucky enough to be under six or over 70, most resorts will let you ski for free. Many will let over-65s ski free. Ask.

Here's an early-bird savings plan. A number of Vermont areas let everyone ski free at the beginning of the day, usually between 8 and 9 a.m. This is called the Milk Run. Dress warmly.

A few Vermont areas have instituted a discounted Sunday morning ticket. It allows you to ski from the moment the lifts open to noon or 1 p.m., giving you time to get back home and catch up on all the work you've neglected since Saturday morning. Currently, Pico and Haystack offer this option. Call ahead to make sure before you turn up at the window demanding the cheap(er) ticket you read about.

The skier who most needs to save cash is the first-time skier. To try out a sport you're afraid you'll hate, you're forced to rent skis, boots and poles, buy a lift ticket, and pay for a lesson. That's an expensive way to discover you'd rather be bowling.

But, if you're a Vermonter, it's no longer necessary. Thanks to a plan pioneered in Vermont and now spreading nationwide, Vermonters skiing for the first time or trying it again after a long lapse can rent, learn, and ski free. Once. To get in on this free introductory offer, call your local mountain and make a reservation for "Discover Skiing, Vermont." On Sunday afternoons, January through late March, virtually every major area in the state offers new skiers this complimentary introduction to the sport, complete with free lift tickets, lessons, and equipment rentals. Once.

In the last five years, some 15,000 potential skiers have tried it. Most of them never went back to bowling.

For up-to-the-minute information on skiing discounts, contact individual ski areas or the Vermont Ski Areas Association, P.O. Box 368, 26 State Street, Montpelier, VT 05601, (802) 223-2439.

Chapter 20

Learning to Ski

I'*ve never skied before — what's the best way to learn?"*

That's a more complicated question than it sounds. It's like choosing a ski resort — the best for one is not the best for all. Here are some of the alternatives ...

The fastest way to learn to ski is to hire a private instructor and ski together all day, every day for a week.

"That's the fastest way?"

That's not only the fastest way, it's by far the most expensive way. Private instruction currently runs about $30 an hour.

"Now let's see — there's seven skiable hours in a day and seven days in a week ... hmmm. What's the cheapest way to learn to ski?"

The cheapest way to learn to ski is this; find skiers you like the looks of and follow them down the mountain, imitating everything they do. The imitation method is free but slow. That's what I did, and it took me 25 years to make a decent parallel turn.

"Twenty-five years? Um, is there anything between a week of private lessons and 25 years in a snowplow?"

Yes there is. If you have limited funds or limited time, here's what I recommend.

First, if you are a Vermonter, call a Vermont ski area and make a reservation to try "Discover Skiing, Vermont!" on the first available Sunday. Lesson, lift, and rental are all free. Then, if you hate the sport and never want to try it again, you've saved yourself a lot of time, money, and frustration.

If you're not a Vermonter, pay for rentals and that first lesson. Then, if you sense there's something in this mad activity that touches a madness in you, arrange a five-day package at the ski area of your choice. Make it a midweek package if you can. Mid-week prices are lower, lines are shorter and classes are smaller.

Make sure your package includes daily lessons. And make sure you take them.

"How do I choose the mountain to spend that first week?"

Use three criteria. First, find out how good the ski school is. In fact, most are good-to-excellent these days, so you shouldn't have too much trouble on that score. The best way to find out about a particular ski school, other than trying it for yourself, is to ask friends who have taken lessons there how it worked out for them. You can also request their instructor. But don't be too disappointed if Karl or Tanya is off teaching racers the week you're there. They move around a lot.

"Is it important who I get as an instructor?"

Yes. And on the first day the school will assign you one who is teaching skiers of your level. Establishing a good relationship with your instructor

is important both to your degree of pleasure and your speed of learning. So if the first one doesn't work out, by all means, ask to try someone else. Most schools should be happy to mix and match.

"What about the children?"

Kids learn faster than adults if the learning is geared to having fun. If your kids are taking lessons, choose a school that is set up to deal with young skiers. Ask the area about children's programs when you call for reservations. Get details about on- and off-snow activities. Find out if classes are given for your progeny's age level. Then make your choice.

The second criterion for choosing an area at which to learn to ski is snowmaking capacity. In times of heavy natural snow, this isn't wildly important, but in lean years there's a big difference between learning on snow and learning on ice. Snow makes it easier to turn and easier to stay vertical, and it's much easier on your body when you become temporarily horizontal. (When you're learning to ski, it's reasonable to expect periods of temporary horizontality.)

Third — and this should probably be first — try to figure at which area you're likely to have the most fun. See the Introduction to this book for suggestions.

For further advice on getting ready for ski learning, ask the Vermont Ski Areas Association for their useful booklet for beginners. They're at Box 368, Montpelier, VT 05602.

Finally, when you're at the ski area and actually taking lessons, you can speed the learning process and dramatically increase your pleasure if you'll do one thing — talk to your instructor.

Tell her what you want to learn. Tell her what you're having trouble with. Confess what makes you afraid. Open your heart and admit your dreams of glory. In short, com-mun-i-cate.

Chapter 21

Snowpiking through Vermont

Vermont amply rewards the winter traveler who takes the time to get off the beaten track.

The state is full of unusual people, curious museums, historic architecture, delightful shops and, of course, spectacular scenery. It's a place where unexpected delights are just around the next bend.

Although skiers come to Vermont primarily to point their skis down mountains, there is more to life here than the perfect run. Because the state is small and its roads well maintained even in the snowiest winters, the pleasures of the unexpected are usually just a few miles from your ski resort. To best experience them, before your trip ask for maps and information from the Vermont Travel Division, 134 State Street, Montpelier, VT 05602, (802) 828-3236. During your stay, ask locals for their recommendations. Then choose a direction, and go snowpiking.

The possibilities are many, from the shops of small cities like Brattleboro and Bennington to the resort stores of Manchester, Stowe and the valley towns of Waitsfield, Warren and Moretown. There are many opportunities off Interstate 89 in Burlington, Waterbury and Montpelier. There's the Golden Triangle area between Bromley, Stratton and Magic Mountain, the many shops of Middlebury and Rutland and the fun of exploring Vermont's many other small towns and cities, from Randolph to Bradford, St. Johnsbury, Newport and St. Albans.

But before you start the car, consider this: most out-of-staters make two serious mistakes when driving in snow. The first is they go too fast. Take your cues from the cars with the green Vermont plates. They aren't dawdling; they're driving at safe speeds for snowy conditions. Follow their example and experience the pleasures of slow driving. Remember, you came here to relax.

The second most common winter driving mistake is trying to steer and brake at the same time. It can't be done. When you need to stop, pump the brakes, don't stomp on 'em, and if you have to make a quick turn, keep your foot off the brake pedal while you're doing it.

Finally, to best enjoy the scenery and have a safe trip, clean all your windows and lights well before you start. It's hard to see through snow.

Where should you go, and what should you look for? Here's a sample destination, easily reached from three northern ski areas: Smugglers' Notch, Jay Peak and Stowe. It goes by that most common American name, Johnson, and it's a good example of the interesting Vermont places you can find.

The town of Johnson is about 15 minutes east of Smugglers' Notch on Route 15. It has one post office, one hardware store and one eating spot, officially called Persico's Plum and Main Restaurant. Whatever it's officially called, the restaurant is known to all locals, now and forever-

more, as the Johnson Diner. It's the kind of place where a large order of French fries will feed a small family — and make them never want to eat at McDonald's again. In fact, it's an ideal place to try French fries the Vermont way, generously dousing them with white vinegar instead of ketchup. Good, by crimus!

Up the road from the diner is Johnson Woolen Mills, ancestral home of the red plaid hunting jacket. Their retail store is the rare, real thing — a factory outlet in the front room of the factory. Jackets, pants, blankets, kilts — they're all on sale in this hundred-year-old factory of a firm that has been in the wool trade for a century and a half.

Up the hill from the mill is Johnson College, part of Vermont's state college system. The college is a center for environmental and recreational studies. Surrounded by the Green Mountains, it possesses the finest view of any college in the Northern Hemisphere. The view alone is worth the steep climb.

Down at the foot of the hill is the Vermont Studio Center, well-known art school and gallery. Artists come from all over the country to study and teach here, and the gallery is open year-round.

Back on the main road, go left at Route 100C and drive west a few miles to the barn-red home of Vermont Rugmakers. Here hand-loomed rugs are made, sold, and sent to homes, offices and embassies around the world.

Johnson's architecture is well preserved 19th century, small-town New

England. You'll find an antique shop or two, a lawyer working out of a old village house, a supermarket and, just to remind you what century you're in, a satellite-dish store. At the north end of town is a public spring from which flows pure Vermont water.

What's extraordinary about Johnson and a hundred Vermont towns like it is that there are a hundred Vermont towns like it. For unlike Weston or Woodstock or Manchester, Johnson is in no way a tourist town. The buildings are preserved because people work in them.

Most Vermonters consider Johnson kind of ordinary. And that's one of the beauties of Vermont — what is accepted as everyday here is well worth a visit.

Chapter 22

Name That Mountain!

Although all Vermont ski areas share the same basic characteristics — mountains, lifts, lodges, trails — these do not add up to a uniform character.

Real differences exist among areas. Some are physical: mountain A is a thousand feet higher than mountain B; resort C's base lodge is three times bigger than resort D's. Other differences are more subtle, but they're sharply enough defined so that any moderately knowledgeable person could distinguish between areas.

If you were that person and had been delivered blindfolded to a Vermont ski resort, by careful looking and listening you should be able to figure out just where in Vermont you are.

Let's test the hypothesis. Here's a brief description of three areas. You decide which ones you're skiing.

• Standing on the top of this cold and beautiful mountain, you notice at once that at least half the people stopping to admire the view are speaking French.

• Skiing beneath the chairlift on a Tuesday in early January, it strikes you that almost every chair is empty. The slopes are nearly empty, too, except for a group of extremely hot young skiers who flash by you for the third time today.

• Although the quad chairlift is state-of-the-art, the clientele is old — not in age, but in money. At this resort, the crisp winter air is filled with the confident smell of inherited wealth.

Let's see how you did. The first mountain is also the northernmost in Vermont and the nearest to Montreal. That accounts for the French accents that add a Gallic charm to the experience of skiing Jay Peak.

Empty slopes and hot young skiers? You're at the only major ski area in the state you can rent all to yourself for the price of a lift ticket. The hotshots are from nearby Burke Mountain Academy, training ground for America's finest racers, and you're skiing Burke Mountain.

Old money on a new lift? Darling, we're at Stowe, of course. Where else would one be?

When characterizing a ski area, bear in mind that character can change. Okemo used to be identifiable by local accents and by the fact that everybody in the liftline knew everybody else. Not any more. Okemo is challenging Killington for the title of biggest and best — big mountain, big lift system, big spenders.

Other areas take great pride in their never-changing character. If you're surrounded by Serious Skiers who take their skiing talk as seriously as their skiing ability, you have to be at one of Vermont's most challenging mountains, Mad River Glen. Mad River's always been this way, and it shows every intention of remaining so forever.

Now, back to the quiz.

• Once again you're at the top of the mountain, and once again you notice strange accents all around you. But this time the vowel sounds are straight out of New Yawk City, right?

• It's winter break time, and when you pass through the village gate, you get the impression that you are entering the Land of the American Adolescent. Most of the people strolling by seem to be fun-loving college students and, judging from the school names on their sweat shirts, they come from colleges all over the East.

• A long and winding access road leads you to yet another country; this one might be called Familyland. Singles and couples are in the minority here; nearly everyone you see has 2.5 children in tow.

Here are the answers:

Those New Yorkers are naturally attracted to one of the two major Vermont mountain nearest them in time and distance. That's why they've schlepped up to Mt. Snow again this winter.

When you find yourself surrounded by college students having an Awesome Time, you know it's winter break, and you're at Smugglers' Notch. Far out!

While driving Ralph and the kids up that access road to Familyland, be sure you have good tread on your snow tires. Oh yes, Familyland also goes by the name Bolton Valley.

We have time for one last question. Ready?

• After a pleasant day on the interesting but limited slopes, you suddenly realize that you're at the only ski area you've been to this year where everybody — everybody — speaks with a Vermont accent.

The answer is you're skiing Lyndonville or one of the half-dozen other strictly local slopes in the state (See Chapter 17). They're not only locally patronized but locally owned and run, often on a volunteer basis. They offer some of the cheapest and most accessible skiing in Vermont.

Vermont Superlatives Quiz

Ok, quizaholics, this is the moment to astonish your friends with your vast knowledge of Vermont ski areas.

Ready?

CATEGORY I: The Beginners' Slope

1. The biggest area?
2. The highest mountain?
3. The longest trail?
4. The oldest area?

CATEGORY II: Intermediate Terrain

5. The snowiest (natural snow)?
6. The snowiest (machine-made snow)?
7. The northernmost?
8. The southernmost major area?

CATEGORY III: Advanced Skiers Only

9. The easternmost?
10. The westernmost?
11. The longest season?
12. The fastest growing?

CATEGORY IV: Double Black Diamond

(prices subject to change)

13. The highest base elevation?
14. The most expensive major area (peak-season day ticket)?
15. The cheapest major area (single-day ticket)?
16. The widest trail?

CATEGORY V: Pub Lawyers

17. The toughest?
18. The least crowded major area?
19. The most innovative ski school?
20. The very best, Numero Uno?

ANSWERS

1. Killington (How big? Very big.); 2. Mt. Mansfield (4,393 feet); 3. Killington (10 miles); 4. Mt. Tom (1934); 5. Jay Peak (300 inches a year); 6. Killington; 7. Jay Peak; 8. Haystack; 9. Burke Mountain; 10. Middlebury College Snow Bowl; 11. Killington (usually mid-October through June 1); 12. Okemo; 13. Bolton Valley (2,150 feet); 14. Stowe; 15. Haystack, Magic and Bromley (all half price midweek); 16. Stratton's Sunriser Supertrail (700 feet at its widest point); 17. Mad River Glen; 18. Burke Mountain; 19. Smugglers' Notch in the North, Bromley in the South; 20. See Introduction, "How to Choose the Best Ski Area for You."

Older's Law

1. Never ride a new lift during its first week of operation. Never *ever* ride one on its maiden voyage. (If you need to ask why, see Chapter 14.) There are lots of folks out there who want to be the first to try a new lift. Let them.

2. Despite what your mother told you, don't wear scarves when you go skiing. Scarves and lift equipment don't mix because if they should mix . . . well, remember what happened to Isadora Duncan. Wear a mask or neck gaiter instead.

3. Your mother was right about hats, though. Unless it's warm out, wear one. They not only provide insulation for the part of your body from which heat easily escapes, they keep your head dry when it's snowing, thus preventing the big chill caused by evaporation.

4. Try not to let your fast friends talk you into skiing over your head. Trust your instincts and the trail signs instead. Sheer terror is not an aid to improved skiing.

5. Neither is excruciating pain. If something hurts — and nine times out of ten that something is feet — get off the mountain and have your boots checked.

6. Speaking of checked, that's what you should have done to your bindings at the start of every season. Yes, even if you only skied three times last year. Weight changes, age changes, level of skill changes, and all these changes affect binding settings. Look upon the annual check-up as, well, an annual check-up.

7. But don't turn down the settings of your bindings in the fall. That used to be a good idea, but materials have improved in recent years, and it's no longer needed or recommended.

8. When you store your skis at season's end, iron a big, sloppy coating of wax onto their bottoms and edges. There's no better protection against dehydration and rust.

9. Between lessons and instruction books, competitiveness and hard-headed determination, it is astonishingly easy to forget the reason you started skiing in the first place. The reason was to have fun. Even more astonishing, when you remember to have fun, your improvement rate skyrockets. So have fun.

Further Reading

ALPINE SKI BOOKS

Adler, Allen. *New England & Thereabouts — A Ski Tracing.* Netco Press, 1985. Copies available from Netco Press, P.O. Box 106, Barton, VT.

A valuable account of the history of early skiing in New England, eastern New York and southern Quebec. Replete with anecdotes and photos, many of which would be lost forever without a book of this sort. Like many home-productions it would have benefited from an independent editor or clerk of the works — a story told in Chapter One gets retold in Chapter Five — yet it's a book worth owning.

Berry, I. William. *The Great North American Ski Book,* 3rd edition. Charles Scribner's Sons, New York, 1984.

Think big. Think 471 pages of skiing history, locale, equipment, instruction and competition. Highly opinionated, sometimes wrong (especially about Vermont skiing and winter driving), always lively, it's a good read. In one form or another, *T.G.N.A.S.B.* has been in print since 1958.

Chamberlain, Tony. *A Critical Guide to Alpine Ski Areas of the U.S. and Canada.* Stephen Greene Press, Lexington, MA, 1988.

"The 72 best downhill areas in North America" says the cover, and although he misses a few, Tony Chamberlain makes a good stab at it. Twelve Vermont areas are covered, each with a black-and-white trail map and a short page of description.

Cochran, Barbara Ann and Lindy Cochran Kelley. *Teach Your Child to Ski.* Stephen Greene/Viking Penguin, New York, 1989.

Solid advice for parents who want to teach their 3- to 10-year-olds themselves. The Cochran sisters are part of Vermont's most famous alpine skiing family.

Enzel, Robert G. *The White Book of Ski Areas.* Annual, Inter-Ski Services, 1988. Available from P.O. Box 9595, Friendship Station, Washington, D.C. 20016.

The White Book is the bible of the ski industry, providing information on more than 700 ski areas from Alaska to North Carolina. Produced annually, it gives up-to-date prices, services, trail information, travel guidance and more.

Gallwey, Timothy and Bob Kriegel. *Inner Skiing.* Bantam, NY, 1985.

Any book about skiing that is dedicated to Guru Maharaj Ji "with growing love and devotion" and which has remained in print since 1977 must be saying something. It does. *Inner Skiing* is filled with good advice that complements rather than duplicates more formal instruction books. It reminds you that skiing is pleasure, not a mid-term exam.

Goodspeed, Linda. *Pico: The First 50 Years.* 1987, available from Pico Ski Resort.

Far better than the average local history, but then Linda Goodspeed is a far better writer than the average local historian. Clear writing, clear photos and a stunning cover.

Hagerman, Robert L. *Mansfield: The Story of Vermont's Loftiest Mountain,* 2nd edition. Phoenix Publishing, Canaan, NH, 1975.

An illustrated history of the mountain, from geology to legends, first ski descents to first balloon ascents, Nosedive to Smugglers' Notch. Great historical photos and a lively, quirky text.

Leocha, Charles. *Skiing America: A Comprehensive Guide to Skiing America's Best Resorts.* World-Leisure Corporation, Boston, annual.

Regularly updated, *Skiing America* offers candid, first-hand looks at North American ski resorts from Maine to California. Six Vermont areas — Killington, Mount Snow, Stratton, Stowe, Sugarbush and Mad River Glen — are described in the current edition.

Passavant, Tom and James R. Peterson. *Playboy's Guide to Ultimate Skiing.* Playboy Press, New York, 1981.

A honey of a book — great fun, terrific descriptions, outstanding photos. Four Vermont chapters — Killington, Stowe, Stratton and Sugarbush.

Sonnenfield, Martha and Frank V. Snyder. *The Stratton Story.* Stratton Corporation, 1981. Available through the Stratton Corporation.

The Stratton Story is a town history that happens to be about a mountain instead of a town. It also happens to be beautifully bound and filled with handsome color photos. Like most town histories, it's a little too discrete about in-house battles to satisfy the gossip-loving reader, but it does tell everything you ever wanted to know about Stratton and then some.

Tejada-Flores, Lito. *Breakthrough on Skis.* Vintage, N.Y., 1986.

The book's sub-title is *How to Get Out of the Intermediate Rut.* The author, who is one of the country's most creative ski writers, tells you just that. Highly recommended.

Weber, Robert E. *The Greatest Ski Resorts in North America.* Guidebook Publishing, Dallas, 1989.

The author only found one greatest ski resort (Killington) in the entire East. He's apparently looking for more in the next edition.

NORDIC SKI BOOKS

Caldwell, John. *The New Cross-Country Ski Book,* 8th edition. Stephen Greene Press, Lexington, MA. 1987.

The book that introduced many Americans to cross-country skiing in the 1960s is updated to include new developments in the sport. Caldwell's wealth of knowledge, his informal, friendly style and love for nordic skiing are un-diminished.

Elman, Raymond. *A Critical Guide to Cross Country Ski Areas.* Stephen Greene Press, Lexington, MA. 1987.

The author describes the 31 New England X-C ski areas he considers the best. He includes trail maps and a useful profile of each area and ties it up in a nicely written package.

Gillette, Ned and John Dostal. *Cross-Country Skiing,* 3rd edition. The Mountaineers. Seattle. 1988.

Jam-packed with information, suggestions and helpful photographs. Dostal and Gillette write clearly, directly and with panache about cross-country equipment, technique, and attitude.

Goodman, David. *Classic Back-country Skiing: A Guide to the Best Ski Tours in New England.* Appalachian Mountain Club. Boston. 1989.

Where to go and what to do when you ski off the beaten track in the snowy hills of New England.

Parker, Paul. *Free-Heel Skiing.* Chelsea Green Publishing Company, Post Mills, VT. 1988.

Parker shows you the secrets of Telemark and parallel techniques on three-pin bindings in all conditions. Full of easy-to-follow imaging techniques that bring you through the turns, from beginning to advanced levels. An articulate, comprehensive manual, complete with advice on equipment.